Lessons Learned
the Hard Way

ALSO BY NEWT GINGRICH

To Renew America

Window of Opportunity,
with Marianne Gingrich and David Drake

1945,
with William Forstchen and Steven Hanser

Newt Gingrich

Lessons Learned the Hard Way

A PERSONAL REPORT

HarperCollins*Publishers*

*Dedicated to Marianne; Kathy; Jackie;
my mother-in-law, Virginia; and my mom, Kit.*

HarperCollins books may be purchased for educational, business, or sales promotional use. For information please write: Special Markets Department, HarperCollins Publishers, Inc., 10 East 53rd Street, New York, NY 10022.

FIRST EDITION

Designed by Elliott Beard

ISBN 0-06-019106-6

98 99 00 01 02 ❖/RRD 10 9 8 7 6 5 4 3 2 1

Contents

Acknowledgments

As readers of this book will recognize, I owe a lot of thanks to a lot of people. My wife, Marianne, my daughters, Kathy and Jackie, and their husbands, Paul and Jimmy. My Republican colleagues in the House and Senate; former Republican National Committee Chairman, Haley Barbour; Ken Duberstein; Dan Meyer; Ed Kutler; Tony Blankley; Vin Weber; and Bob Walker. Bob Dole has been such a staunch friend and advisor. Lady Margaret Thatcher has been a source of inspiration, strength, and advice. My extended family has been a wellspring of help and emotional support, especially my mother, Kit Gingrich; my mother-in-law, Virginia Ginther; my sisters; brother; in-laws; and their spouses.

I am eternally grateful to the countless Georgians who have always been there for me—and without whom none of this would have been possible. While there is not room to list each of them here, their friendship and support mean more than they will ever know. I only hope that I have added even half as much meaning and inspiration to their lives as they have to mine.

My life has been enriched by friends all across America, especially Gay and Stanley Gaines, Michael and Janet Berolzheimer, Owen and Susan Roberts, Shelly and Lynnie Kamins, Tucker Andersen, Terry and Mary Kohler, Bo Callaway, and all my supporters at GOPAC, Friends of Newt Gingrich, and Monday Morning who make our busy schedule possible.

I am supported by a wide range of very hard working and conscientious people, including Rachel Robinson, Heather Hopkins, Sonya Harrison, Mark Peterson, Ginny Williams, Christy Surprenant, Jack Howard, Lisa Nelson, Christina Martin, Dave Ryan, Mike Shields, and Scott Rials.

I lean almost every day on Joe Gaylord, Nancy Desmond, Steve Hanser, and Arne Christenson to advise me and help make my activities effective.

I also could not go without special thanks to two close friends who also serve as my lawyers, Randy Evans and Ed Bethune.

In recent years Terry Maples, Edward O. Wilson, Michael Novaceck, and Jack Horner have rekindled my love of the natural world and my fascination with life in all its forms.

Finally, Adrian Zackheim's editing and Midge Decter's guidance, advice, and friendship have made this a much better book.

CHAPTER 1

LEARN TO LEARN

ON THE DAY BEFORE THANKSGIVING 1994 I was driving in Georgia with my wife, Marianne. We were in a state of high excitement. Just a couple of weeks earlier the Republicans had received 9 million new votes, the largest increase for one party in American history. As a consequence we were looking at the first House Republican majority in forty years.

There had for some years been a new feeling in the country. People had grown seriously weary of liberalism and all its works, from a swollen and counterproductive welfare system to an ever-worsening public education system to a breakdown in public manners and morals. It was this feeling that had elected Ronald Reagan, and it was this feeling, stronger than ever, that had now propelled a whole new group of young conservatives into Congress. It had also propelled me into the Speakership.

One of the ways we had tapped into that feeling and given it a focus was by drawing up the legislative plan we had called the Contract With America. In addition to being fed up with liberalism, people would, we believed, be comforted by the idea that we were not just going to be in opposition but that we had a positive program we were promising to push it through immediately. It turned out that we were right. The voters were with us.

As I was describing all our great plans to Marianne, with my usual boyish exuberance I burst out, "This is a really big change!" She looked at me with a cross between sympathy and disapproval and said, "You don't have any clue how big this change really is."

It would take two and a half years and a lot of pain for me to understand what she had been trying to tell me that afternoon. And as I look back now, I am astonished at how badly I had underestimated the size and intensity of the problems that would confront me as Speaker of the House. I was, after all, not completely inexperienced in the way Congress worked: As Republican whip I had had my share of responsibility for moving things along—or, on the other hand, for keeping them from moving. Nevertheless, far too often in the coming months and years I would find myself unprepared.

Some of this lack of preparedness was to a certain degree excusable. In the first place, there had not been a Republican Speaker of the House for forty years. There was no one left around with the kind of institutional memory that could have helped us in making the transition from being in opposition to being in the position to govern. As we would quickly learn, these two experiences—being in opposition and being in the majority—are vastly different. The election of 1994 had brought to Washington a new generation and breed of congressmen.

They were not ordinary politicians but rather ideologically fervent and determined people. They arrived in Congress very much a unified class, ready to bring about a lot of serious changes. And like me, they were in what turned out to be too big a hurry.

Besides all this, in having won an idea-oriented national campaign without a presidential leader, we were something of a rarity in American history. I believe only Henry Clay and the Warhawks of 1810 and the Progressive movement of 1910 had pulled it off before. All of which is to say that we were involved in a much more significant transfer of power than was implied by a mere shift from a Democratic to a Republican majority. This meant in turn that the Speakership would be an even weightier—and, as it would turn out, even more delicate—proposition than it had normally been.

In short, overnight I found myself in a job far bigger than most people, even Washingtonians, understand to this day. The Speaker is the third-ranking constitutional officer. That in itself might seem weighty enough. In addition, the day-to-day job requires him not only to preside over, but to attempt to lead, 435 strong-willed, competitive, and independent-minded people. (Some wag has likened this to an attempt to herd cats.) After all, if these people had not in the first place been heavily endowed with all three of these characteristics—will, competitiveness, and independence of mind—they would never have been able to get through the process of winning a primary, followed by a general election, followed by the requirement that they represent 600,000 of their fellow Americans in the nation's capital. So if they sometimes made difficulties for one another, and for me, that was one of the great strengths of the system.

All of this added up to the fact that, politically experienced as

I was, everything seemed a little unfamiliar to me. I hadn't shifted from my old job to my new job fast enough. I hadn't shaken off some of the habits I had acquired being the minority whip. I'll give you an example. As the minority party, we were in the position of having to fight every day just to get some media attention. We tended to say and do things that were far more strident and dramatic than are prudent to do and say as the leaders of the majority who find themselves in front of the microphone every day. If you are seldom covered by the press, which was the case with House Republicans for forty years, you have a lot of leeway to make mistakes. But when you are in people's living rooms every evening, your mistakes are magnified.

I should have known this. The day I won the race for whip, I received a call from John Sununu, then President Bush's chief of staff. "As of today you need to change your press operations totally," he told me. "Up until now you had a press secretary to get you into the press. Now you need a press secretary to keep you out of the press." I thought that was a clever insight and believed I knew what he meant. Clearly I didn't. I will have more to say about the challenge of the media in a later chapter, but my early experiences are relevant to the story of my difficult transition.

When I first arrived in Washington as a freshman member of the House, C-SPAN was just preparing to televise House and Senate proceedings. I was sworn in in January 1979. The following March the cameras went on. Seeing the educational possibilities in having at least some of the work of the Congress broadcast to the country, I began to work overtime, along with my colleagues Bob Walker, Vin Weber, and Connie Mack, to use this medium.

For a long time Congress had been taking a backseat to the

White House where press coverage was concerned. There were various reasons for this. For one thing, during World War II and the Cold War foreign and military affairs had been a major preoccupation of the national news, and these had largely been the business of the Executive. For another, Sam Rayburn, longtime and legendary Speaker of the House, the very model of a traditional senior legislator, had consciously tried to minimize public attention to the work of the House. No doubt he viewed it as a potential difficulty for his very old-style ability to make deals and control votes. But by January 1995, when the new Contract With America class was being sworn in, the amount of congressional media coverage had expanded immensely. In addition to C-SPAN, there was now CNN, a twenty-four-hour-a-day news channel, a daily *Congressional Quarterly* bulletin, and two "local" newspapers, *Roll Call* and *The Hill*. In short, we now had a giant screen and loudspeaker to catch all our missteps and misstatements. Looking back I can see how magnified they would come to be—and how convenient for our opposition.

The truth is that the transition from my old job as whip to my new role as Speaker took too long and was too costly.

Ironically, one reason I was such a slow learner was that things were going so well. Dick Armey, the majority leader, was doing a marvelous job of running the House day to day. We had promised to fulfill the Contract With America in one hundred days, and the process was going like clockwork. Bob Livingston, chairman of the Appropriations Committee, cut $53 billion from the appropriations accounts. (This was the first time in modern history that someone whose job was to appropriate had actually *dis*appropriated on this scale, and his having done so remains one of the unsung feats of heroism of the 1995–97 Congress.) Indeed, all the chairmen were running their committees well. John Kasich was engaged in an effort that would produce the first balanced budget plan in a generation exactly according to schedule. We had a Medicare Reform Task Force, led by Congressmen Bill Archer, Tom Bliley, Bill Thomas, and Mike Bilirakis, that, together with an unprecedented kind of cooperation between the Ways and Means and Commerce committees, was creating an entirely new proposal for saving that overextended and endangered system.

Precisely because things were going so well in the first six months of my speakership, I too, like Medicare, began to get overextended. Instead of slowing down and focusing on what we needed to do each day, I kept enlarging our ambitions and trying to force things to happen on too many fronts at the same time. As for myself personally, in addition to presiding over the House, I was teaching a course, writing *To Renew America*, finishing a novel, and of course giving speeches, press interviews, and holding press conferences. It was all too much.

I was of course not the only member of the 103rd, and later the 104th, Congress who was loaded for bear and had things to learn. The House Republicans arrived fresh from their 1994 victory with enormous élan and excitement, ready for immediate action. The word "revolution" was in the air, and everything from government spending to health care to welfare was waiting to be turned around. On the House side of the process many of the reforms we were after were proceeding rapidly, but we were soon to learn why President George Washington once described the Senate as the cooling saucer into which the hot coffee from the cup of the House should be poured. By its very nature, as intended by the Constitution, the Senate can be excruciatingly slow to move.

Historically, change comes into being first in the House and—perhaps—over time moves into the Senate. The process was designed to happen that way, for the Senate is meant to be a line of defense against dictatorship or mob rule. This idea goes back to the way senators were originally elected: by the state legislatures rather than directly by the people, which helped to insulate them from popular passions. The Founding Fathers had been very conscious of the dangers of demagoguery and mob rule that are the inevitable threats to freedom in a purely democratic system. They tried to arrange it so that the senators represented only the interests of their respective states and not those of the populace. Indeed, for its first six years, the Senate actually met in secret.

In this sense, Robert Byrd is the most classically senatorial of all modern senators—with Jesse Helms a close second—and if you read Byrd's *History of the Senate* you can see how passionately he holds to a belief in a careful, often obstinate, and if need be even cantankerous process of senatorial negotiation. He has, of course, received a lot of criticism for being what many people would call plain obstructionist, but I have come to believe that he is more in the right than they. If an idea isn't good enough to survive a couple of really tough fights in the Senate, maybe it isn't worth implementing after all.

Be that as it may, every new representative has a lot to learn about the ways of senatorial obstruction. For example, any individual senator can put an item on hold without having to explain why. While this usually doesn't by itself kill a piece of legislation, it can slow the process to a snail's pace. In the end a senator is likely to be very careful about insisting on a hold, because a fellow senator can do the same to something he or she cares about. There is what you might call a balance of legislative fear, which makes the process of negotiating in the Senate very different from that in the House. Still, senatorial prerogatives are jealously guarded, and in dealing with the Senate, one always has to look out for them.

Once, for instance, we tried to do something as seemingly unobjectionable as get permission to bring the Ringling Brothers circus elephants onto the Capitol grounds. The idea was that we would bring the animals on, welcome the circus to Washington, and thank the circus for its program of outreach to poor children. When he got wind of this, one senator, who shall be nameless, decided to put our request on a personal hold because he didn't think it was right for elephants to be kept in circuses. By the time Bob Dole was able to unlock the resolution, almost a month had gone by and we were within two days of having to cancel the visit. Such are the vicissitudes of legislating in Washington, especially when the Senate is involved. I'm not sure that that was quite what George Washington had in mind by a cooling saucer, but it was certainly part of what everyone who wishes to make things happen in Washington has to learn.

Beyond the ability of a senator to slow things down through the use of the personal hold, at every step of the way there are senatorial hurdles to overcome. In the committees, in the procedures on the floor—including the possibility of a filibuster—and probably above all, in the conference committees in which the House and the Senate try to settle their differences over a bill—there are many potential pitfalls.

Nor did all this exhaust the forces arrayed against us. In early '95—that is, almost immediately after the excitement of our victory at the polls—we were to learn the hard way that there was a difference between having a Republican majority and having a *conservative* majority. It was true that conservatives had a majority among the House and Senate Republican members, but this was not anything like a majority of the House or Senate. There were about 170 solid conservatives in the House and 46 or so in the Senate, and the fact was that the margin of our majority status was made up of partisans who shared our Republicanism but not necessarily either our conservatism or our activism. We were so filled with confidence about what we could accomplish that we badly underestimated what we were up against. After forty years of minority status, every success in scheduling and passing legislation through the House was positively exhilarating. As a result, we were not prepared for how long and difficult the process of turning our bills into the actual law of the land was going to be.

Nor had we conservatives taken the measure of how reluctant certain important senators were going to be about going along with certain key aspects of our agenda. For instance, one big disappointment for the conservatives was our failure immediately to eliminate the National Endowment for the Arts. Certainly any listing of the most bizarre and extreme misuses of taxpayer money would have to include such examples of NEA artistic grants as that to a certain HIV-infected homosexual "performance artist" whose art consisted of cutting his uninfected fellow performer onstage and dangling the blood over the audience so they could experience the risk of contracting AIDS, or to two professors standing at the Mexican border and handing out $10 bills to illegal immigrants as they cross over into the United States, and so on and on. Everyone has his own favorite cases. There is no question that if the majority of ordinary Americans were to see many of the examples of where NEA money goes, they would favor abolishing the system. Yet in the Senate there has always been strong support for the agency, for the NEA also supports such things as opera, ballet, and art museums, and the major private donors to such honored arts institutions are also major supporters for senators. In any case, the social pressure of the elites—and what is better loved by the elites than the arts?—has always been felt more strongly in the Senate than in the House. This is one example among many, but despite all these constraints and difficulties, Bob Dole as majority leader managed to get an amazing amount of the Contract With America through the Senate.

We had other lessons to learn as well. We had not only failed to take into account the ability of the Senate to delay us and obstruct us, but we had much too cavalierly underrated the power of the President, even a President who had lost his legislative majority and was in a certain amount of trouble for other reasons. I am speaking of the power of the veto. Even if you pass something through both the House and the Senate, there is that presidential pen. How could we have forgotten that? For me especially it was inexcusable, because when I was Republican whip during the Bush Administration one of my duties had been precisely to help sustain presidential vetoes. President Bush vetoed more than thirty bills and only one was overridden.

Looking back, I now see that some part of the problem of our having overlooked the power of the President had to do with the way we had begun to define—or perhaps I should say, had not begun to define—our strategy. A legislator and an executive are two very different things, and for a time we had allowed ourselves to confuse the two. The point is best illustrated by the story of a truly exciting session we had in December 1994. With us then were our new freshmen, the cause of our being in the majority, and all of them raring to go. We had invited Governor John Engler of Michigan to speak to us on the floor of the House. It was an electrifying moment for all of us. Engler told us how he had taken on the issues of welfare reform, lowering taxes, and cutting back on the bureaucracy and fought to get his policies instituted in the teeth of massive hostility from the press and the unions. Ultimately he had succeeded, his program had been passed, Michigan's economy had improved dramatically, and he had won a stunning victory. It's hard to describe the enthusiasm he aroused. But certain of the wiser old heads who were present pointed out that Engler had a four-year term of office and thus had a good deal more time to recover politically than the House Republicans would have if they ended up in a fight to the end with Clinton. Every member of the House faces reelection every two years. That is a very short time to take a pasting from all your opponents and regain your ground. What they were really saying, perhaps without putting their fingers precisely on the problem, was, Aren't you basing yourselves on what is actually an executive rather than a legislative sense of reality?

In any case, as anyone who reads newspapers or watches television news knows, between the hostile press coverage, the bad polls, and the advice (and complaints) I was receiving from my allies in the House, reality had begun to move in on me with a bang.

The final blow was delivered to me not, as you might expect, by some piece of hostility but rather by an act of true friendship. On February 4, 1997, as we were getting ready for Clinton's State of the Union address, Senate majority leader Trent Lott, a friend of twenty years' standing, dropped by my office. He came to give me a few tips on how to sit properly and look presentable. He told me I should wear a certain kind of shirt, and that I should lean forward so as to minimize for the camera how overweight I had let myself become. I was bathed in embarrassment: Things had obviously gone pretty far downhill.

To be fair to myself, I had been required to lead a far from healthy and normal life. In addition to my responsibilities in the House, during the previous four years I had been traveling without stop: For the '94 election, I had campaigned in 140 districts, and for the '96 election, in 130, and in addition I had been running around helping to raise money for both the Republican National Committee and the National Republican Congressional Committee. This is no recipe for staying in shape.

If Trent had not been so good a friend, it might have taken me longer to come to my senses. In any case, then and there I vowed to diet and exercise . . . and a whole lot more.

CHAPTER 2

LEARN TO LISTEN

IF YOU ARE SPEAKER OF THE HOUSE during a time of immense change, it is a good idea to think about the help one needs to create a genuine political transformation in a democracy (the twentieth century has given us all too many vivid examples of transformations of the other kind).

Under ordinary conditions when everything is going along as usual, a leader needs to think about and handle only what is on his or her plate day to day. They must work hard to make the right tactical decisions and support the right policies and people, but they can comfortably accept what they have inherited in the way of a power structure. In other words, their interest will be in running the system effectively, not in changing it.

Thus, almost by definition a leader engaged in trying to bring about a transformation will find himself living in an environment hostile to his intentions. The system he is trying to reform, after all, is the established one. The old order, as old orders always do, will be fighting for its life and thus will be engaged in undertaking everything possible to stop any new system from emerging. If the leader of an intended transformation relies on the information and judgments made available to him through the various means established in the old order, he will invariably find himself making the wrong decisions and doing the wrong things. Thus he must keep his vision rightly focused, his will fully engaged, and his self-discipline intact.

Margaret Thatcher, a prime example of what I mean by a transformational leader, was from the very first moment of coming to power fully aware that most of the establishment of her country (and even of her own party) was opposed to her policies. Her response to this first of all was simply to ignore the media. She had a firm rule that she would not read anything negative about what she was up to because it might weaken her morale and distort her judgment.

She also had a very keen sense of how long it would take and how difficult it would be to engage in the process of transformation. I sat with her in December 1996, and the first thing she said to me—as if she could read my mind—was "Don't expect this year to be easy. It took three years for them to get used to the idea of my being Prime Minister, and the third year was the worst. I expect you will have one more difficult year, so don't lower your guard." Since we were right at the edge of the ethics wars which would come close to ending my career, her comments were not only prescient, but in retrospect were also a profound spiritual help. Through the whole coming year I drew strength from them.

Ronald Reagan had a similar knack for ignoring his critics. I have always suspected that this was a talent he developed when he was making all those B movies. The *New York Times* movie critic was hardly enamored of Ronald Reagan films (with the possible exception of *King's Row*), but the public kept buying enough tickets to keep him something of a star. He also began to cultivate friends from the conservative movement, especially in California, and he came to read *Human Events* and *National Review* far more carefully than he did *Time* or *Newsweek*. He was concerned about the America he knew and loved and about the ideas of the movement he had made his own. And—as his years as governor of California gave ample proof—he felt neither threatened nor moved by what the liberal academics, or later the Georgetown social set, had to say against him.

In short, the key to a successful transformational leader is to keep your eye focused on your goals and your ear tuned to your friends. I studied Reagan's and Thatcher's experiences in office, and had the opportunity to talk to both of them (especially after they retired); and in addition, I was able to interview a number of people who had worked closely with them. And then, as I said before, there was the great instruction to be found in history. I have studied the transformational leaders of the past, most especially among them Andrew Jackson, Abraham Lincoln, Theodore Roosevelt, Woodrow Wilson, and Franklin Delano Roosevelt. Not all of them, of course, transformed things in the same way or to the same degree, but from every one there was something important to learn.

When I first arrived in Washington as a new congressman from Georgia, I came with a number of goals that would have struck most observers as the ambitions of a fantasist if not an outright megalomaniac. For instance, I wanted to participate in bringing down the Soviet Union at just the moment when my fellow Georgian Jimmy Carter had declared us cured of our "inordinate" fear of Communism while the Soviets were on the offensive everywhere. Then, too, I wanted to build a Republican majority in Georgia at a moment when there were no other federally elected Republican officials from Georgia. (After two defeats, I would in fact be the only one. Now eight of the eleven House members and one of the two senators from Georgia are Republicans.) I dreamed of helping to elect a Republican majority in the House when there had not been one in twenty-four years, and at the time of which I speak, would not be one for another sixteen years.

I wanted that Republican majority to be a certain kind of majority, one based on ideas. I also wanted it to represent a party that would be open and beckoning to a majority of our fellow Americans not because we were handing out goodies to people but because we had better proposals for them and their families' futures. In short, I wanted to do nothing less than replace the welfare society with a society full of opportunity. I dreamed of a society that would begin to move the powers of a smothering, overcentralized federal government back to the states and local governments and into the hands of volunteers much closer to the people and better aware of their real needs and wants. And I wanted to accelerate America's move into the information age so that we could have an advantage over the rest of the world both in commerce and in defense.

Not exactly a small order. It would take nineteen years of slow, steady work by a lot of dreamers, first in Georgia, then in the House Republican Party, then in the House itself, then in the federal government, and finally in the Republican Party all across America. The key to those years was to keep focused on what I dreamed of bringing about for the country in general rather than on the liberal city in which I was spending most of my working life. For remember: To work in Washington is to wake up each morning surrounded by the *Washington Post*, the *New York Times*, the national television networks, National Public Radio, lobbyists who even if they are personally conservative are focused only on who's got the power today, the Washington bureaucracies, and the Washington social scene. From the time you wake up until the time you go to bed, unless you take steps to defend against it, you are bombarded with opinions, signals, and agendas that are antithetical to a conservative's own.

There were periods when I would have to brace myself to pick up the *Washington Post* in the morning because I knew what awaited me. There were articles sure to depress me and my fellow conservatives and designed to keep us off balance. There have been times when I have simply refused to read a newspaper because I knew it would just demoralize me. During the periods when I found myself most engaged in conflict, I would adopt the Thatcher rule and simply live through the fight until it was over. I found that the more selectively I read the papers or watched television, the more energy and optimism I felt. Ultimately I often gave up watching the weekend interview shows as well because they displayed so much pettiness and hostility that it simply wasn't productive. I doubt if I watch them more than once a quarter now, and frankly I don't miss them. As a few of the figures who appear on those shows have grown ever more self-important, they have in equal measure grown less useful to learn from. I am, naturally, happy to appear on those programs, but I don't often watch them. If something important happens on one of them, my press secretary will brief me.

For the same reason, I find that I seldom watch television news. If I do, it is usually on CNN or the Fox channel—sometimes MSNBC—generally, as it happens, when I am exercising.

Not that I am not kept apprised about what is going on. Members of my staff keep me informed during the day by walking into my office with stories that merit my attention as they break on the wire. Beyond this, when Marianne and I are driving any distance in our car, we listen to Rush Limbaugh on the car radio. He is a good friend. He also makes good arguments and is amusing. In Atlanta I will occasionally listen to Neil Boortz, because he is also a good friend, with a wicked gift for argument. But in truth I don't often get to listen to talk radio, because most days my time is totally preempted by meetings and preparing for speeches and just keeping up with the work on my desk.

None of this is intended to give the impression that I am not mindful of the media and the grave problems and tremendous opportunities they create for keeping one's hand on the pulse of the country. Take the case of the opportunity presented to us last year. One of President Clinton's aides declared that the scandals then surrounding the IRS were not a real problem. Within an hour we released to the press a letter to the President in which we expressed our concern for the White House's indifference to the anxieties of the taxpayers. We insisted that the IRS must be reformed and that taxpayers' rights as Americans be protected. By the next morning, the White House was in full retreat.

Be all that as it may, and though the media can sometimes be tools rather than stumbling blocks in moving the government to a recognition of what the people need from it, usually the best policy is to go about your business without allowing the media to distract you.

Which is probably just another way of saying that a transformational leader has to be sure of what he wants to happen and extraordinarily strong-willed in seeing that it does. Leaders, remember, are not always in the right of things. Winston Churchill, for instance, was just as clear in his mind and just as strong-willed when he was wrong about the Indian Empire Act and the retention of Edward VIII on the throne of England as when he was fatefully so right about Hitler and the significance of radar. Naturally, the leaders we remember from history are those who were right about very big things and kept sight of them no matter what happened.

As I have said, one of my deep commitments through the years before 1994 was to help the Republican Party become a majority in the House. Among other things, it seemed to me very unhealthy for the country to have a one-party monopoly of legislative power. Much of what I did—as you have probably already realized—I tried to keep harnessed to this particular end.

One of the things I love to do is read the documents left behind by the historical figures who one way or another shaped our world: General Eisenhower, George Marshall, Churchill, and so on. The first thing that strikes one in all of their papers is how briefly and with what clarity each of these men was able to communicate his intentions and instructions. One particularly striking document is a memo written by Eisenhower rather early on in World War II, in which he sternly insisted that those responsible for the conduct of the war keep in mind the distinction between the necessary and the desirable.

Determining what is necessary as distinct from what is desirable is a lot harder than it sounds. I would guess that in a whole adult lifetime of trying, I myself have probably succeeded only 20 percent of the time. Which means that maybe 80 percent of my time and energy has been spent not on the necessary but only on the desirable. But even a focus of only 20 percent of your time and energy on real goals is probably more than most people attain. One of the tricks here is brute repetition, getting up every morning with one thing in mind while others are busy with a whole variety of passing impulses.

All this becomes doubly important if the city you are getting up in is one dominated by your ideological opponents. They will be trying to distract you from your own concerns and focusing instead on theirs. If you are going to keep them at bay, you must never let up for a minute in the discipline of keeping your own objectives in the forefront.

There are not too many better examples of the importance of keeping your eye on the ball than the story of the drafting of the Interstate Transportation Bill in the fall of 1997. To most readers the inside story on a number of other issues might seem more fascinating than the story of the drafting of an interstate transportation bill, but in this case most readers would be wrong. This bill went to the very heart of current politics, and how it was written into law speaks volumes about the political state of play in this country. The bill governs the funding for federal highways and mass transit, and as such is of enormous importance to every single state, and every governor of every single state in the Union. No matter how ideologically conservative they are, when it comes to highways and mass transit, state and local officials all have their eyes on the money. Their argument is that the federal gasoline tax is a user fee; all they want is a return of the money to the citizens who paid it. Whatever the merit of their argument, the point is that even in a conservative Republican Congress the pressure for more transportation spending is enormous.

Transportation spending has yet a further wrinkle: To wit, historically there have been donor and donee states. The donor states were those who paid more in gasoline taxes than they got back, while the donee states got back more than they paid in taxes. Given the length of time that the Democrats controlled Congress, the states with big cities and mass transit systems tended to be donees (Michigan being an exception), while the more conservative West and South tended to have donor states. Trying to break this tradition would prove to be a difficult and complicated proposition. The donor states are 60 percent of the votes in the House, while the donee states were stronger in the Senate. There was the danger that a bill which came close to retaining the current formula, while it would pass in the Senate, would require big modifications to pass in the House. So Bud Shuster, chairman of the Transportation and Infrastructure Committee, reasoned (correctly, in my view) that he could not solve the problem simply by taking money away from the donee states. That would cause an unsustainable degree of practical and political pain. He needed to figure out how to hold the donee states harmless while adding new money to the donor states according to a formula whereby every state would get back at least 95 percent of the money it had paid into the transportation trust fund. Shuster and his team put a great deal of serious work into gathering support across the country, and in the end produced not only a strong bill but one with a deep base of support.

There was only one problem: The bill provided for more spending than was allowed by the budget agreement. A powerful argument could be, and was, made by Shuster and the members of his committee for the need for this high level of spending. Despite the budget agreement, the highway trust fund was going to have more than enough money. First of all, there was now a substantial amount of user-fee (gasoline tax) money being paid into it. Second, we had helped Shuster's case by negotiating in the budget agreement to have the money collected from Clinton's 1993 gasoline tax increase of 4.3 percent paid into the trust fund rather than into the general treasury, where the liberal Democrats had used it to help pay for welfare state spending. Since this money would now be put where it had always belonged—in the trust fund to pay for highway and mass transit systems—there would be billions more to spend on transportation infrastructure. Still, the budget agreement had set a specific cap on transportation spending. It would spend less than the trust fund had in it. The new bill shattered that limit.

This all began to bubble in early September 1997, barely a month after the President had signed the balanced budget agreement into law. We were in real danger of looking like a bunch of fools or hypocrites if we turned around and brought out a massive multibillion-dollar, multiyear bill that destroyed the very spending ceilings we had just written into law.

To make matters even more complicated, the underlying economic forecasts and government spending and revenue forecasts were almost month by month making the budget agreement obsolete. With each new forecast, the deficit for fiscal 1997 (from October 1, 1996, through September 30, 1997) was shrinking. In January 1996, the Congressional Budget Office had forecast a deficit of $140 billion. By spring of 1997, when we were negotiating the budget, it had shrunk to $60 billion. One night in the middle of our negotiations—we had in fact just about finished negotiating—the Congressional Budget Office forecasters were estimating an improvement of $225 billion in their deficit projections for the next five years. All our calculations were thrown for a loop, and we were happily forced to renegotiate a whole series of items in the light of our having come so much closer to a balanced budget. When the President signed the balanced budget law in early August (ten months into the year the CBO was trying to estimate) the projection was still for a deficit of $35 billion. When the fiscal year ended two months later, the actual deficit turned out to be $22.6 billion. That, of course, helps keep interest rates low, since the government had to borrow $100 billion less than had been predicted.

Our goal, of course, had always been to balance the budget by the year 2002. When we first adopted this goal, it seemed like an impossible dream. Now we were faced with the possibility that we would realize our ambition even before 2002.

To return to the dilemma of the Transportation and Infrastructure Committee, it maintained that it could finance its highway and mass transit bill with the new budget numbers and still get to our original goal of balance by 2002. Technically, the committee was clearly right. The problem was that we would not be adopting a new budget until the spring of 1998, and to allow the committee to break the budget barrier for its purposes would set a precedent for every other committee, which would be able to make the same argument. The balanced budget process would die of a dozen exceptions, and our most powerful achievement would have been destroyed by our own members while President Clinton took the credit as the defender of the balanced budget agreement. He would veto the highway bill, and we would end up not only without a balanced budget but without the needed investment in transportation. So I met with Bud Shuster and the members of his committee and explained our dilemma. After a series of discussions, they agreed to wait until the spring of 1998. If at that time the deficits had continued to decline, the entire House Republican Conference would take part in the decision as to how to apportion the money. Some would undoubtedly want all the money to pay down the national debt. Others would want it to go for tax cuts, and still others would advocate that some of it should go to modernizing such critical national priorities as defense, science, and transportation.

I have told this story about the transportation bill because it seems to me to sum up so perfectly the kinds of pressures experienced by House Republicans. On the one hand, the prospect of having to deal with a generation of surpluses, happy though it is, is so unprecedented (not since the 1920s have we had even the possibility of living without deficits) that we will have to have a very broad and full debate just to focus our minds on what to do about it. On the other hand, we will also have to be constantly vigilant to be able to stay within budget year after year. We will be under constant pressure to buy just one more item than has been budgeted for, and after all, every serious interest group in the country can make a case for the need to spend more. Imagine the temptation for politicians, who are after all only flesh and blood, to please certain of their voters by seeking just one more exception to the agreed-upon cap on spending. In a way, we shall have to be just as focused and vigilant—perhaps more focused and vigilant—in maintaining balance than we have had to be just in establishing the very principle of balance. It would have been so easy—which is why I told this story in the first place—just to have made an exception of Shuster's meritorious bill. In the light of the country's experience over the past six decades, this is, as I have said, a happy problem. But it is a problem all the same. Thanks to the understanding of our whole team that a tactical victory might be a strategic defeat, we still have the possibility of achieving all our goals—balancing the budget in 1999 and building highways within a new budget agreement in the spring of 1998.

In Washington, with all its day-to-day pressures and lack of sufficient fresh air for the mind, one needs to take time, preferably every morning, just to think about what is going on and what one should be doing about it. Some withdrawing every weekend, into books, say, or just seeing a movie, can be essential to clearing one's head. I think people not involved in the life of the nation's legislators would have difficulty understanding what a torrent of pressures it really is. From dead center of this torrent I have, in the past few years, been required week by week to figure out what a whole group of people will be required to do and in what sequence they will be required to do it. Without some opportunity to think and talk things through quietly with friends and advisers and colleagues, I would, I think, have burned out long ago.

The House, as you surely have seen by now, is neither a corporation nor a military institution. Not only do we not have a rigid hierarchy, we do not have a defined orderly process of management. This makes a certain clarity of mind not only important but essential. And sometimes, even when you know what you are trying to accomplish, you can't figure out where it is supposed to fit in the overall plan for success. At that point you must shift from the immediate situation to reminding yourself of your higher and larger purpose—in other words, to refocus on your values and goals. Then you will know how to complete your immediate task with those in mind.

For example, one of the key values of most conservatives is opposition to tax increases. This is not only right in itself, but helpful as well, because it protects us from all sorts of temptations that the liberals so love to place before us. Conservatives are elected by taxpayers who believe they already pay too many taxes, who want smaller and more efficient government, and who wish to be able to keep more of the money and property they have earned by the sweat of their brows. They feel betrayed when their own leaders are maneuvered into supporting bigger and ever more intrusive government by agreeing to raise taxes. If they wanted that, they could have voted for the liberals in the first place.

Another related value is the commitment to maintaining a balanced budget in peacetime. This is more than a matter of taxation. It is based on the belief that our very moral order requires adherence to the principle that no generation has the right to spend its children's and its grandchildren's money. This principle in turn reminds citizens to live within limits and not to look to government as an unlimited tool of public policy.

And where I personally am concerned, one other very important principle is being able to explain what we are doing when we go back home. Washington is a city full of very clever people who have wonderful schemes as long as these schemes can be kept out of the public eye. One of the great weaknesses of the former Democratic majority was its increasing propensity to have hidden meetings of unnamed experts who developed plans that could not withstand the light of day. For example, in one Congress, they combined passage of a big tax increase with a proposal for a government-run health care system and a costly liberal crime bill. As former Congressman Gene Taylor of Missouri said, "There weren't enough wagon tongues to stand on in order to explain all three of these measures in the average congressional district." By trying to do more than they could explain to the American people, the Democrats forfeited the right to control Congress. If the Republicans were to get correspondingly cocky, we would once again be creating an opportunity to serve in the minority.

The principle of keeping the people in on it all the way is my contribution to the great tax reform debate. Some intelligent and persuasive people want a flat income tax. Some other intelligent and persuasive people want to see a sales tax replace any income tax. Yet other intelligent and persuasive people believe in a modified flat tax that retains certain deductions. Each of these groups provides a plausible argument for its own proposal, and I am intrigued by all of them. So my own goal in the great tax reform debate is to make sure that it is carried way beyond the experts and advocates and gets a thorough airing in the minds of the voters. I want them to tell me what they think about this question. In other words, I want what public opinion analyst Daniel Yankelovich calls the coming to public judgment. Yankelovich makes a truly useful distinction between public judgment and public opinion. The latter is what people tell pollsters off the tops of their heads. Public judgment, by contrast, is what develops over time when people pay attention to something and discuss it with their friends and neighbors. It takes a long time to develop and involves a complex social interaction that is largely unplanned and unprogrammable. Public judgment is deep, solid, and unlikely to change in the absence of some new and large external event.

Take the case of the Clinton health care plan. When it was first unveiled it was greeted with fairly strong support in public opinion. The President gave a good speech to a joint session of Congress, and the news media gave him days of solid supportive coverage, including interviews with a lot of people who favored the plan. By the end of the first week the polls indicated that the plan would go over big. Eight months later this same plan turned out to be a huge liability for the Democrats. It was, indeed, a major reason why they lost the 1994 elections. Some liberals, to be sure, argued that the defeat of the health care plan was the result of a huge advertising campaign against it by the health insurance industry. One of the hardest things for liberals to accept is that their core belief in centralized bureaucratic government and the government redistribution of wealth has fewer and fewer adherents in the society at large. They keep seeking alternative explanations for the popular rejection of their ideas, including, if necessary, the assertions that people are just greedy and selfish or that they are racist. In the case of the Clinton health care plan, the plan was beaten because after people had had the chance to pay some serious attention to it, they didn't like what they were hearing. In the short run, the public can perhaps make things difficult, but in the long run they are the best and most stable and most reliable judges of what they truly want and need.

For my own part, one of the things that keeps me from being carried off by the Washington whirlwind is my lifeline to a lot of people like my daughters who are in far better touch with everyday life than someone in my position is permitted to be. I also keep the skull of a *Tyrannosaurus rex* in my major meeting room as a reminder to myself of how shallow and frail is the human ego. In the middle of some hot clash of wills I look over at T-rex (on loan from the Smithsonian and mounted with its formidable jaws open) and imagine that 65 million years ago that dinosaur was wandering around the North American continent looking for something to eat and thinking that it was important. In addition to T-rex, on my bookshelf is a copy of Franz de Wahl's *Chimpanzee Politics,* which is a wonderful study of the social and political interactions of the chimpanzee colony at the Arnhem Zoo. No one who reads his description of chimpanzees maneuvering for status and power will ever again watch humans with quite the same seriousness.

I would strongly urge anyone who wants to work in Washington to keep close contact with friends outside the city. That is one of the key values of travel outside Washington. The first thing I discover when I call people outside Washington, for example, is that they are paying attention to things that have nothing to do with legislative strategies or executive-legislative struggles or anything of the kind. They are thinking about getting their children off to school, or looking forward to holidays, or planning vacations, or running their businesses—in sum, generally keeping busy in happy, productive ways that have absolutely nothing to do with the Washington power struggle and that keep them on the whole in a far better mood.

Another thing I am reminded of is that people lead their lives on a human scale. We talk about billions and trillions. We debate whether to bomb Saddam Hussein. Most people think about what is close to home, about their friends and their kids' friends, about losing their jobs or paying off their mortgages or planning family celebrations—whatever is part of life lived at an intimate level.

Things in the world look very different at that level. When the Bush Administration tried to convince me that a gasoline tax increase would be okay and would barely be noticed, I tested the theory with two phone calls. First I called my mother-in-law in Leetonia, Ohio, and then I called my older daughter in Greensboro, North Carolina. My mother-in-law is a retired woman, at the time aged seventy-five. She has a lot of friends who live on limited retirement incomes, and driving happens to be one of their pleasures (the Sunday afternoon drive is still a major American recreation). She was personally against the idea of a gasoline tax increase, and she thought the idea would go down very badly with her friends. Then I called my daughter Kathy. She runs a small business, and her husband is the tennis coach at the university. Her reaction was, to put it mildly, scathing. "What planet do they live on?" she asked. She thought such a tax increase was the very antithesis of why people had elected the Republicans. After those two conversations, any doubts I may have had simply vanished, and I opposed the tax increase.

My daughter Kathy helped me again three years later when the new Clinton Administration was having a hard time with Zoe Baird, Clinton's nominee for attorney general. Readers may remember that this nominee had twice hired illegal immigrant workers as housekeepers and had failed to pay social security taxes for them. As it happened, Washington's Georgetown set included a lot of people who had employed illegal immigrants as maids and had also not paid social security taxes for them. Around Washington the general attitude toward this problem with Zoe Baird was forgive and forget; after all, everybody does it. Among some of my own business supporters, however, as I learned at a breakfast meeting, there was a feeling of anger at the idea that the chief law enforcement officer of the United States should be someone who had consistently broken the law, and over a considerable period of time. I left the breakfast and called Kathy at the Carolina Coffee Company. What did she think about the Zoe Baird problem? This time she was really angry rather than scornful. She herself had both an Argentine and a Russian working for her, she told me, and in both cases she had insisted on seeing their green cards (their legal entitlement to work in the United States) before she would put them on her payroll. Second, she paid the social security tax both on them and on herself before she took a penny of salary. She believed without question that if she had attempted to do what Zoe Baird had done, the Immigration and Naturalization

Service and the IRS would have carted her off to jail.

An hour after this conversation I held a press conference calling on the President to withdraw Zoe Baird from nomination. I figured that Kathy was undoubtedly representative of a lot of small businesses, and they deserved to be spoken for. A week later I was out for an early morning walk, and a Republican senator jogged past me. He stopped, turned around, and came back. "Thanks for giving all of us a wake-up call," he said. "We were all sleepwalking until we saw your press statements on Friday." Later that day the nomination was withdrawn. The point of this story is not how I helped to stop a bad nomination, but that when I called for her advice, my daughter the small-business owner had been able to be the voice of small business and, I believe, the voice of most law-abiding citizens as well.

The trick is not only to call but to listen.

Ronald Reagan knew about the priceless value of listening to people, and among other things it enabled him to find the winning issue in the 1966 California governor's race despite all the best efforts of all his professional advisers and consultants. He needed, to be sure, to prove that he was not just a movie star. His advisers decided that to prove his mastery of detail, they should hold town-meeting-style question-and-answer sessions with groups of voters. They carefully prepared for a wide range of questions. Reagan rapidly discovered that the most commonly asked question had not been included in the prepared material. This was the time of the so-called free-speech movement in Berkeley, and people were getting ever more upset with the student radicals. At every meeting, this was what the people wanted to ask Reagan about. Reagan's people decided that it was not really a gubernatorial issue and advised him to dance around it. Characteristically, Reagan understood his audience better. If this was what they felt passionately about, this was what he would discuss with them. By his third meeting he had an answer he could deliver with strength and clarity, and the line between him and his too-soft opponent Pat Brown was drawn.

Reagan would have the same experience again in 1976, when he was running against Gerald Ford for the Republican presidential nomination and had lost badly in several primaries. Some experts thought his political career was all but over, until in North Carolina he made a speech in opposition to the Panama Canal treaties. No consultant would have advised him to talk about foreign policy in North Carolina, but from talking to people Reagan knew that the issue of the Panama Canal was not about foreign policy, it was about such things as national pride and honor. This was post-Vietnam, and the conservatives were ready to hear someone speak again about America's pride and America's interests; and the Panama Canal speech was so powerful and so successful that it effectively relaunched the Reagan presidential campaign and brought him within a few votes of the nomination against a sitting Republican President. And the rest is history.

In sum, true political transformation requires a leader to keep his eye always on the ball and his ear very, very tuned to the people.

CHAPTER 3

LEARN TO KEEP
YOUR MOUTH SHUT

Air Force One

A LONG TIME AGO, THE VERY wise and practical Don Rumsfeld—former Secretary of Defense and chief of staff to President Gerald Ford—offered what seems to me the ultimate useful advice. "If something can't be changed," he told me, "it is a fact, not a problem. It's what you do about it that is a problem." I no longer remember what in particular occasioned his saying this to me, but I can't think of anything to which it can better be applied than the relations between the media and the conservatives.

Now, though officials of the media insist to this day that it is not so, every honest citizen in this country knows that the people who produce television, films, and most of the major daily newspapers are overwhelmingly liberal. After all, every poll of the Washington media shows overwhelming support for liberal Democrats. I must confess that though the reasons for this have been explained to me many times, deep down I will never understand why so many of America's most honored journalists should be on the left. Still, there is simply no denying that they are. Nor can anyone deny that while conservative ideas—not to mention conservative politicians—have been growing ever more popular among the voters over the past quarter-century, they are treated with a special kind of hostility, if not downright ridicule, by most of the institutions of the media. Talk radio, of course, is a happy exception, because it is more open to citizen participation.

People may have noticed that in recent years I myself have often been the object of what can only be called a very special measure of media attention. For one thing, of course, no matter what you are, to be in power is to be news. If you are not only in power but conservative, the press's scrutiny is usually both intense and hostile. In fact, if I had been of a mind to in the years since 1994, I could probably have spent a major portion of each day just answering all the mean and distorted things I got to read and hear about myself. But that would not only have been a pointless and wasteful way to spend my time, it would also have turned out to be highly pleasing to the very people who would like to see me gone from the scene—and with me, the ideas and policies that my colleagues and I represent.

I have to admit that in my time I have given the journalists more than a few unnecessary opportunities. Often when I have done so it's because I have lost my cool or I've been feeling very happy about something. Believe it or not, I grew up with a strong personal bias in favor of reporters. My natural inclination is to like them. I was conditioned that way as a teenager under the influence of a dear friend and mentor named Paul Walker, who published a weekly newspaper in Harrisburg, Pennsylvania. I also enjoy—as you will see, sometimes too much—getting into lively exchanges with them. I may be over this particular pleasure by now, but some part of me needs to learn over and over again that they are not on my side.

Take what happened to me on election night in 1994. I was—hardly surprisingly—feeling pretty exuberant. Even so, for several hours I gave a series of carefully thought-out and responsible television interviews, in which I talked about such politically proper subjects as keeping our promises in the Contract With America, our hopes for being able to work with the President, and so on. Then, at about 2:30 in the morning, I found myself taking a walk with two reporters, one each from the *New York Times* and the *Washington Post*. They wanted, they said, something in the nature of an "inside" take on my views and intentions.

Now, if I had only had Ronald Reagan in my mind's eye at that moment, I would have told them, "You just heard me say on television exactly what it is I have to say, and have a pleasant evening." After all, any conservative who does not keep in mind at all times that the press has a natural inclination to lean left and favor the Democrats is not paying attention to reality. It is simply a fact of life. Reagan knew that better than anyone and was skilled at dealing with it. I seem to have forgotten it.

Instead, partly because I was so happy, partly because the reporters were so clever, and partly because the history professor in me escaped from the discipline imposed on him by the political leader, I spent twenty minutes giving lengthy detailed answers to the questions that no Speaker-to-be in his right mind should have answered. One of the ground rules for conservatives has to be that the elite press will never cover your message if you give them an excuse to cover anything else. They may not cover it even if you remain disciplined, but at least you won't have done yourself any harm.

Finally they asked me why I thought the Clinton policies had been so badly repudiated by the voters, and if I thought the Clintons were really so liberal. Again, I should have said, "Ask one of the expert analysts; my job is to concentrate on legislating." But what I actually said was that it seemed to me that the Clintons having worked as McGovern activists in their student days was a legitimate clue to their real beliefs, and that these beliefs were also being reflected in a number of the President's appointments. Naturally, the next day both papers ran front-page stories under headlines that read "Gingrich Lobs a Few More Bombs" (*Washington Post*, November 10, 1994) and "GOP's Rising Star Pledges to Right Wrongs of the Left" (*New York Times*, November 10, 1994). And there went all my effort to reach out and establish a good working relationship with the President. There is an old parental saying that nothing good happens after 11 P.M. What was once applied to teenagers (and could apply even more so now, in my opinion) might equally refer to press interviews.

That particular blunder about the Clintons I committed on my own. Nor was it the last or the biggest. It would take me two painful years to learn that "no comment" was very often the best thing to say. Reporters, after all, have the right to ask any questions they want to. For one thing, it's what their editors expect them to do. But we have no obligation to answer them. No comment beats a self-destructive comment every time.

Because we had been so successful in getting our message out before the election, my press secretary Tony Blankley and I still hoped that we might still get at least part of the press on our side. So we decided to hold daily televised press briefings. The daily press briefing was an institution that Democratic Speakers had used for years, but their briefings had been restricted to reporters without cameras. We on the other hand had decided to show how bold and up-to-the-minute media-wise we were.

Now, there were enormous differences between the role of the previous Democratic Speakers and my role. They had been essentially legislative leaders speaking to the press about legislative matters, not many of which were going to make it as page-one national news. Mainly they were explaining the workings of the House to a group of reporters who were experts focused on legislative affairs hoping to get a paragraph or two for some other story or for a Sunday analytical piece. I, on the other hand, was essentially a political leader of a grassroots movement seeking to do nothing less than reshape the federal government along with the political culture of the nation. Thus almost anything I said could be a possible item of front-page news. CNN indicated how important it considered these briefings by carrying them live. That alone should have been the tip-off to us that we were playing with fire. But we plunged on.

It will thus surprise no one to learn that our press briefings turned out to be an ongoing headache. They got to be little more than a game of "pin the tail on the Speaker." I was complaining one day about how hard it was to get anyone to respond seriously to the news we were offering at our briefings when a friend and associate who had once been press secretary to Mayor Harold Washington of Chicago told us the facts of press-briefing life. The members of the press who turn up at these briefings, he explained, are only interested in what they call "gotcha," that is, they were waiting for us to make a slip, any slip, so they could go back to the newsroom and tell everyone how they'd tripped us up that day. As long as we kept putting ourselves out in the open, he said, in an unplanned and unstructured way, we were simply inviting them to try to score off us.

We also did something we should have done from the very beginning, namely, consulted with such Reagan-era communications experts as Mike Deaver, Ken Duberstein, and Mari Will. With the help of our friends and allies, we were finally brought to our senses and closed down the press briefings.

In addition to making real mistakes, where the press is concerned there is also the possibility of being just plain blindsided. When people are actually happy to see you stumble, there is no end to how far they will go to make sure you do it—including, if need be, picking on innocent and trusting elderly ladies.

This was brought home to me on the very day I was to be sworn in as Speaker. I had gotten up very early that January morning, gone to my new office, and stood out on the porch, which overlooks the Mall and which is one of the Speaker's most enjoyable assets. From there I had watched the sky get light, thinking with wonder about the United States and how an army brat from Harrisburg, Pennsylvania, with no money and no connections could end up where I was standing at that moment. Later Marianne and I, together with our families—who had gathered in Washington to celebrate the day with us—attended an ecumenical prayer service at a nearby Catholic church, organized by Congressmen Bill Emerson, Frank Wolf, and Tony Hall. Wolf gave a talk on the subject of reconciliation that was so moving I changed the speech I had prepared for the swearing-in. Soon after that I was back in my office considering the question of how we should go about our business on the first day of the hundred we had promised the American people it would

take us to fulfill our contract with them. Suddenly Tony Blankley walked in looking grim. CBS newswoman Connie Chung
had interviewed my mother a couple of weeks earlier, and it
seemed that in the course of the interview my mother said that I
thought Hillary Clinton was [an unprintable word]. CBS had just
announced that it would all be on Connie Chung's show later in
the week. I was dumbfounded. I knew that Connie Chung had
visited my parents in Harrisburg weeks earlier and that they had
liked her so much my dad had baked her his famous pineapple
upside-down cake. And now this. You can imagine my mother's
mortification at having caused me trouble and put a crimp into
what should have been a wonderful day for all of us. My father
was doubly angry. As a regular army man he had always been
suspicious of the news media, but in response to Connie Chung
he had let his guard down. Now he felt that he had been sucker-
punched. I didn't know what to be angrier about, the hostility of
CBS in putting out this teaser just in time for what should have
been one of my happiest days, or Connie Chung's having taken
such advantage of my inexperienced mother by means of a little
naked manipulation. If you look at the full tape of the interview,
you see Connie Chung saying, "Why don't you just whisper it to
me, just between you and me," and my mother leaning forward
and whispering in what she really imagines is an intimate
moment. It may be fair game to play "gotcha" with an experienced politician—though even so, I'm not sure just what contribution it makes to the common good. But to pick that way on a
friendly and trusting elderly woman bursting with pride at the
achievement of her son is just plain dirty in my book. Later,
when the show was broadcast and people could see with their
own eyes how Connie Chung had used my mother, public sentiment turned decisively against the newswoman. In the end, my

mother and I apologized to Mrs. Clinton, and she graciously accepted our apologies and invited my mother to tea.

Though my family and I overcame this particular sneak attack—and anyone who has ever been subject to one can tell you how the experience reverberates in one's nervous system—it would take a good deal more unpleasantness of this kind before I learned what was most important about conservative dealings with the press: that, in and of themselves, they are of secondary importance. We have to learn to speak over the media and around them as well as through them to reach our true audience, who are the ordinary people of this country.

Sometimes, indeed, I think we conservative politicians and officials tend to forget how much the people "out there" are with us. The age of liberalism is over, and millions upon millions of ordinary Americans are in effect calling on us to figure out how to replace it without too much disruption. We do in fact know how to do that, though people go on needing to be convinced that there will be no unmanageable hardships for them concealed in our plans.

They need something else as well, especially from us. They need to believe that we understand how people feel. This is sometimes an uncomfortable thing for Republicans to make convincing. Often we tend to talk as if we are a group of managers analyzing some problem in a boardroom. Democrats, on the other hand, whatever their other shortcomings, have a passion for both power and people and instinctively know how to focus in on both. You might say that they on the whole come on like a party of lawyers making an appeal to a blue-collar jury, while Republicans come on like a party of managers making an appeal to a board of directors. Guess who is more successful at mass communication?

Still, we are learning what is perhaps the single most important lesson of mass communication: Living, breathing people will always be more interesting than a narrow focus on ideas every time. If you want to explain to the public what is wrong with some current government practice or, on the other hand, what is right with some new initiative, find someone who humanly embodies what you are talking about and ask him or her to speak for you.

For example, when we wanted to explain to the public the kind of damage being wrought by America's trial lawyers with the types of lawsuits in which they basically just blackmail some industry or other, we invited a very sick young girl to testify about certain biomedical materials that were saving her life and that would no longer be produced if the company were subjected to class action lawsuits. Or when we were pushing for scholarships that would enable inner city children to attend the schools of their choice, we held a press conference featuring a welfare mother from Cleveland, Ohio, who, thanks to Governor Voinovich's program, could now send her children to a safe and academically successful school.

The principle involved here, of course, is not only simple but obvious. Just sit yourself in a room full of people, any kind of people, and see what happens when a baby is brought in. Whatever they were talking about before, their minds are all concentrated on that baby now. It is in fact one of the nice things about people that normally our primary interest is in one another. Republicans, as I indicated above, are now learning to use this basic lesson about communication—at least in creating what might be called press "moments" to illustrate our policy initiatives.

But television has its own special requirements as a medium of communication, and I in particular had to learn and relearn one basic lesson in dealing with it (a lesson, by the way, I should

have learned thirty-five years ago from reading Marshall McLuhan).
Television creates a very intimate connection between you and
your audience. For one thing, it brings you very close to people,
and for another, it brings you into their own living rooms and
bedrooms and kitchens, where they are relaxed and comfortable.
If you come across as angry, strident, or hostile (what McLuhan
called a "hot" personality in a "cool" medium), you inevitably jar
people and make them uncomfortable. All too often in my television appearances I would focus too intently on the challenges
being thrown at me and end up too passionate, thus allowing
those hostile to me to look through a twenty-minute interview
and pick out the twenty seconds when I was angry.

Television technique aside, there is finally no better example
of the trouble you can bring down on your own head when you
forget the press is always ready to pounce. I look back on the
story I am about to tell as the single most avoidable mistake I
made during my first three years as Speaker: Call it the saga of
Air Force One.

I was at a fund-raiser for one of my favorite projects, Habitat
for Humanity, when I heard that Israel's Prime Minister Rabin
had been assassinated during a peace rally in Tel Aviv. Marianne
and I had known him for several years. We had visited him in
Jerusalem and had recently entertained him at the Capitol in cel-
ebration of Jerusalem's three thousandth birthday. We were
shattered. As soon as I got home I called the White House and
offered to do whatever I could to help. I was told that the President wanted the highest-ranking delegation possible to attend
Rabin's funeral and was asking Senator Dole and me—and
because she had known Prime Minister Rabin and cared deeply
about the future of Israel, Marianne as well—to accompany
them.

We jumped on a plane and flew to Washington and joined the President and his party on *Air Force One*. The flight to Israel, as you can imagine, was a very quiet and somber affair. The President stopped by briefly to chat on the way to Tel Aviv. After the funeral and a series of intense meetings with Israeli government officials and politicians, we returned to *Air Force One* for the trip home.

As it happened, we were at that moment in the midst of budget negotiations, and I expected that at some appropriate moment Bob Dole and I would be invited to sit down with the President and chat about how we might work together to solve the budget problem. This was the kind of opportunity for Clinton that FDR or Lyndon Johnson or Ronald Reagan would have grabbed in a heartbeat. I had been on trips with Reagan and George Bush and knew how powerful a mechanism that plane could be for inducing you to work with the President. As the hours went by, the Democrats were being invited to the front of the plane for chats, and Bob Dole and I were not. Well and good. I was having a fascinating time chatting with former Secretary of State George Shultz and Mort Zuckerman (the owner of *U.S. News and World Report* and the *New York Daily News,* about whom more below); and Bob Dole and I had some quiet time for a planning session together. And, it had been generous of the Clintons to invite Marianne along. However, I was puzzled by the President but not deeply concerned.

When it came time to deplane, Dole and I were informed by the White House staff that we would be leaving from the rear of the plane with them. I thought this was bad form, especially for Bob, our senior leader and probable candidate for President, and I couldn't imagine that Bob Byrd and Tip O'Neill would have stood still for some White House staffer giving the brush-off to the Congress in that way. But I saw no point in complaining, and we deplaned as instructed.

A few days later, I was the guest at a Sperling breakfast. The Sperling breakfast is an institution created by Budge Sperling, the *Christian Science Monitor*'s senior Washington correspondent, at which a group of Washington reporters gather with an elected or appointed government official and spend an hour over breakfast asking questions. We were in the middle of the first of the government shutdowns. I was trying to explain how hard it is to do business with the Clinton Administration and why, fatefully, we had in the end been prepared to let funding for the government lapse in order to force a confrontation over the balanced budget. I explained how the President on the one hand said he wanted a budget agreement while on the other hand his party was running utterly dishonest ads about the issue; how on the one hand the President was personally engaged in talking with us about a possible agreement while on the other hand the negotiators he sent to deal with us were very liberal and more interested in arguing ideology than in reaching any mutual understanding.

"Let me give you an example of how hard it is to understand this President," I said. And I proceeded to tell the reporters about what had happened to Bob Dole and me on the presidential plane. If he is genuinely interested in reaching an agreement with us, I said, why didn't he discuss one with us when we were only a few feet away on an airplane? Then, I continued, digging my grave a little deeper, if he wanted to indicate his seriousness about working with us, why did he leave the plane by himself and make us go out the back way? I said it was both selfish and self-destructive for the President to hog the media by walking down those steps from the plane alone instead of showing a little bipartisanship precisely when he claimed he wanted to reach an agreement with us. My reaction, I said, was petty but human.

By now my press secretary Tony Blankley was positively white with horror. He—by the way, I now see correctly—had not expected serious negotiations from Clinton in the first place. He had advocated a more cautious strategy, in what we did and in what we said.

I didn't follow Tony's advice, and the guest of honor at the Sperling breakfast had not been the Speaker of the House. He had been the foolish professor, delivering a freewheeling lecture full of careless and unguarded statements to a press corps that was looking for a sensational angle.

The story exploded almost immediately. Of all the papers, and there were quite a few who put the story on the front page, the worst was the New York *Daily News,* which ran a banner headline on page one that read simply, "Crybaby." Other papers may have been less hostile, but the press attack was only the beginning.

Congressman Charles Schumer, a very smart, very aggressive liberal from New York City, took to the floor of the House waving a copy of the *Daily News.* He proceeded to attack me for putting people out of work just because I had felt mistreated. Naturally, a number of Schumer's fellow Democrats followed suit.

Nor could the White House resist getting into the act. First, Mike McCurry, the President's press secretary, released a photo of all of us talking with the President on the airplane. Actually, the photo was simply a picture taken at a meeting we all had on the way to Israel in which we briefly discussed funeral and security arrangements. Again the Democrats rushed to the floor. For days, their press operations fed on every aspect of the story.

When some reporters challenged McCurry on the photo he released, he said the President had been too emotionally exhausted by the funeral to undertake any serious discussion. Several days later—too late to be of any help—Mort Zuckerman said that on the contrary, the President had been happy and relaxed and had spent several hours with him playing hearts. Zuckerman added that in his opinion it had been a lost opportunity, and the White House should just admit it. This was one of the ironies—albeit in this case a pleasant one—with which my life at times seems to abound: Zuckerman happens to be the owner of the *New York Daily News*, the paper that did the most to embarrass me. Whatever the White House might have done, there was absolutely nothing I could do—no tactic, no clever strategy; nothing but time and a change of subject could come to my rescue. I was sick, and my Republican colleagues in the House, who had to sit by in silence as the Democrats had a field day, were even sicker. All because I didn't know when to keep my mouth shut.

In facing crises of press coverage, it is well for everyone, including me, to remember that American public life has always been a rough-and-tumble affair. Jefferson and Hamilton, for example, actually subsidized newspapers to blacken each other's names. The Jacksonians ran a vicious campaign of character assassination against John Quincy Adams. The anti-Jacksonians, on the other hand, defamed Jackson's wife and marriage, leading Jackson to shoot one of the defamers in a duel. As for Lincoln, he was called every bad name a hostile press could summon up.

In the end, there is nothing you can really do to eliminate this problem. It goes with the territory, a territory that I happen to love, and a territory that is a little less dangerous if you learn when to keep your mouth shut.

CHAPTER 4

PICK YOUR FIGHTS WISELY

Medicare

GIVING UNINTENDED OPENINGS to the press, then, can be a very costly practice. But failing to take the proper measure of an opponent, whether in business or war or politics, can be a far costlier, sometimes even fatal, one. This is the lesson Napoleon was taught by Wellington, and it is the lesson the new Republican House majority was taught—thankfully not fatally—by William Jefferson Clinton. Failing properly to take him into account was something that turned an intelligent policy into an unsuccessful one.

The story concerns that perpetually hot potato, Medicare Part B. Medicare Part B is an optional medical insurance program that covers doctor visits. It was designed to have 50 percent of its costs covered by premiums paid by the insurees. The other 50 percent would be paid by taxpayers. It seems safe to say that this particular aspect of the history of the program is either forgotten by or not known to the majority of people. Over the years the beneficiaries have come to pay a lower and lower percentage of the cost. Finally, the trustees of the Medicare fund reported that since costs were so far outrunning income, within a few years the program would be bankrupt. To add to the problem, Bill Archer, the chairman of the House Ways and Means Committee, pointed out that under current law Medicare premiums would fall automatically if the law wasn't changed. For premiums to actually fall when Medicare was headed toward bankruptcy seemed wrong. This was a technical problem. Everyone agreed that if we were to save Medicare, it would have to be fixed. In addition, we were, of course, trying to balance the budget. It seemed obvious to the technical experts that freezing the share of the Medicare Part B premiums paid by retirees in a continuing resolution would be sound policy. We would add that provision to a larger bill that would keep the government open.

As everybody knows, or should, the special genius of the American Constitution is in the way it balances power. The Founding Fathers had clearly intended for Congress to have a major role in shaping the laws. The House is to originate all tax bills and all spending bills. No money can be spent without congressional approval. But to ensure that there would be balance, the President on his side was given the power to veto any bill, after which it would require the votes of two-thirds of the members of both houses of Congress to override that veto. In the absence of a final agreement between the executive and the Congress about how much money will be needed in the budget, the government is kept running temporarily by a stopgap method of financing called a continuing resolution.

The idea that we should force Clinton into a showdown by tacking something we wanted onto something he badly needed to keep the government in operation grew out of the fact that while Republicans had gained control of Congress, we had not won a big enough majority to override a presidential veto. In fact, we were some sixty votes short of that possibility. However, we thought we had a strategy that would achieve the same effect. If the President would not sign the spending bills we were willing to pass, we would prove equally unwilling to pass the spending bills he wanted to sign.

We were relying on our belief that the majority of Americans wanted a balanced budget and wanted to end deficit spending more than they feared closing the government. If he would not bend to our will and we would not bend to his, there would be a stalemate. The stalemate would in turn lead to a very public and much publicized fight. Once the American people began to pay serious attention to it, they would side with us and bring pressure on the President to agree to our program of cutting taxes, reforming welfare, and balancing the budget.

The idea of a grand showdown over spending had long been a staple of conservative analysis. Even before Reagan's inaugural, he had been approached by one prominent conservative who urged him to force a showdown over the debt ceiling and simply refuse to sign on to one until the Democratic Congress reined in its spending plans. Reagan rejected this idea with a comment I wish I had understood better at the time. "I wear the white hat," he said, "and the man in the white hat doesn't force that kind of crisis." The conservative activist who told me that story was convinced that Reagan would have won such a showdown. For fifteen years I agreed with him, but I was to learn

something about the American people that too many conservatives don't appreciate. They want their leaders to have principled
disagreements, but they want these disagreements to be settled
in constructive ways. That is not, of course, what our own
activists were telling us. They were all gung ho for a brutal fight
over spending and taxes. We mistook their enthusiasm for the
views of the American public.

Now back to Medicare, one of the issues on the agenda of
the great showdown through which we were going to teach
Clinton a lesson, but ended up giving him an opportunity. What
the technical experts, being technical experts, might have
thought was sound policy—namely, holding the Medicare premiums at their current levels—the legislative leaders should have
recognized immediately for what it was. They should have
known that it would almost certainly result in a painful self-
inflicted wound to the Republicans and that, in addition, it
would be an unexpected boon to a President who was at that
time in pretty bad political shape. Medicare is a government program about which almost everyone, especially seniors, feel passionately. For us to block a cut in the premiums, essential as such
an action might seem, would surely be too golden a public relations opportunity for any Democratic President, let alone this
one, to pass up. But we did not think of it this way. We were in
the middle of negotiating with the President, and since he had
said that he wanted both to save Medicare and to balance the
budget, we just assumed he would have to accept our provision
for freezing the premium.

How naïve could we have been? Clinton was our opponent.
Our having won control of Congress had come as a most
unpleasant shock to him. As the legislative branch, we have the
power to initiate legislation. As the President, he has the power

to veto legislation. We have the right to describe a piece of legislation in our way. He has the right to describe it in his way. Then it is up to the public to decide whom to believe.

As it happened, at the time we are talking about—the fall of 1995—Clinton was in deep trouble. His reelection was in doubt. There was a real danger that a liberal would run against him in the primaries, which would have been a potentially devastating setback. Each time a serious opponent within his own party had emerged to run against an incumbent President (Reagan against Ford in 1976, Ted Kennedy against Carter in 1980, Pat Buchanan against Bush in 1992), the incumbent lost the election. Thus it was very important to the Clinton team to avoid being challenged from the left. But though he had to guard his left flank within his own party, to rebuild his strength with the voters out there in the country he had recently been forced to spend his time moving rightward on the issues of balancing the budget, reforming welfare, and reducing taxes. It has become an iron law of politics that a Democrat must move left for the primaries and then move right for the general election, but Clinton was in so much trouble with the public at large that he had had to move straightaway to the general election strategy of moving to the right.

Our decision to go ahead and freeze the Medicare premium merely on the assumption that he would agree and without getting his word on it must have seemed to him a gift from heaven. Here was an issue that would become a rallying point for every liberal in the land, that would rouse senior citizens in droves, and that would give the President the opportunity to sound the old class warfare theme of the Republicans' plans to offer tax cuts to the rich while blocking premium cuts for the poor. And so on.

We had earlier been the victims of this same kind of dishonest claptrap over the school lunch program, but that time its authors had been only the congressional Democrats and their allies in the news media. Moreover, as it would turn out, the public did not buy.

The great school lunch press campaign came to my attention one morning in early 1995, at one of my ill-starred morning briefings. In the course of this briefing one of the reporters asked about the Republican intention to kill the school lunch program. To the best of my knowledge, I replied, pleased with my own calm, there is no plan to kill the school lunches. But that's what we were told by the Democrats, the reporters insisted, and proceeded to repeat the most vicious canards about how the children are starving and the Republicans wish to kill the only means for providing them at least one decent meal. I went to ask Bill Goodling, chairman of the House Education and Workforce Committee, what had prompted the House Democrats to initiate this campaign. He told me that the Republicans were proposing to issue block grants to the states so that the school lunch program could be administered locally, where its needs would be better understood and more efficiently managed. And as far as spending goes, we were actually increasing spending on it—though naturally not by as much as the liberals claimed to want.

If anyone were interested in doing a case study of the disinformation and scare tactics of the left, the school lunch debate would be a perfect example. The high point of the Democratic campaign came when Tom Daschle and Dick Gephardt, who had been assigned to respond to my televised speech about where we needed to go after the Contract With America, had had themselves taped in a school lunchroom. As the camera rolled, they emoted about the plight of the starving children from whom the Republicans were about to take away their only source of breakfast and lunch.

Daschle and Gephardt and the congressional Democrats overshot: People could see the value in having the states look after school lunches. Unfortunately for us, this would not be the last time Democrats used demagoguery.

When it came to the issue of Medicare, that was a different matter, one that could so easily be used to engage the fears of the elderly. Looking back now I can't understand how we could once have been so naïve about the Clinton Administration. What we proposed to do made perfect sense to anyone who wanted at one and the same time to save Medicare and balance the budget. True, the President had said he wanted to do both, but we went ahead without his explicit agreement.

The orchestration of a well-conceived, full-blown, presidential media campaign can be a wonder to behold.

First, Clinton and Gore begin to intone a mantra, which would be repeated daily for a whole year: "We wish to save Medicare, Medicaid, education, and the environment," while, on the other hand, the Republicans "intend to cut taxes for the rich while they ruthlessly and heartlessly go about cutting funding for Medicare, Medicaid, education, and the environment."

There are two fascinating doctoral dissertations to be done on the $40 million public relations campaign to which we were subjected, one on the number of times in the course of the year the President and Vice President and their surrogates were able with a straight face to repeat that mantra, and the other on the 80,000 questionably or possibly illegally financed negative advertisements that were at the same time being run all across the country.

For us Republicans in Congress, one of the most impressive aspects of this assault was the way Democratic activists in the House and Senate could be counted on to march in lockstep with it. The Democratic Party, of course, is much more of a political machine than the Republican Party. Those members of the House who had switched from the Democratic Caucus to the Republican Conference—there have been something like a dozen of them—kept remarking how surprising they found the lack of intimidation and groupthink in the Republican Conference. They were not used to it. But the Republican Party does after all tend to recruit individualistic entrepreneur types, and we pride ourselves precisely on being a conference rather than a caucus. Sometimes to our sorrow, we expect our members to disagree with us.

I do not mean to suggest that the Democrats in Congress never disagree with one another or their leadership, but at that point they had been pretty shattered by the experience of finding themselves in the minority for the first time in forty years. They had for one thing lost their committee chairmanships, which is all by itself a tremendous loss of power and prestige, and they were quite out of the habit of taking a backseat. They were absolutely determined to win back a majority, and this determination fused them together into a very partisan and very aggressive team. So whatever their own opinions, they too spent the year chanting the President's mantra.

As I said before, we should have recognized going in that the President had the power to defeat any initiative on our part to alter the status of Medicare. His veto led us to accept the decline in premiums, and it further weakened Medicare. We should not have touched the program without securing some prior agreement from him. In addition, by that time we should already have learned that no matter how well Clinton might recognize the need to take some action, if there was any personal political advantage involved, he would cheerfully deny that he had ever recognized anything of the sort. Finally, we should have known—something we had learned in fact during the Reagan Administration—that at least at first, the White House media operation trumps any effort of that kind by the Congress.

If the Medicare initiative had ended up being nothing more than a great public relations opportunity for Bill Clinton, what can I say about the case of the great government shutdown?

In 1995 we were, understandably, feeling very high as a result of our great victory. The President, on the other hand, seemed to be in a good deal of trouble. In the first two years of his administration he had made bad appointments, pushed through the largest peacetime tax increase in history, and capped it all off with an extremely unpopular try at creating a system of government-run medicine. Moreover, he and others in the White House seemed to be implicated in various scandals and were potentially in danger of trouble with the law. To our minds nothing better signaled his newfound feeling of weakness in the face of our electoral sweep than his decision to move to the right. Suddenly he was embracing—or at least speaking as if he were embracing—a good deal of our legislative program.

People feeling confident of their own strength often fail to take the proper measure of their opponents. That was certainly the case with us and the President. Had we done our homework about this man, especially about his career in Arkansas, we would never have been quite so confident of our ability to push him into signing our legislation into law. This was a man who had lost a congressional race, bounced back to become Arkansas attorney general, been elected the youngest governor in the country, failed to win reelection, then became governor again for four terms. Next he ran for President against an incumbent George Bush, who, coming off a very popular war, for a time had had very high approval ratings. Though in the early summer of 1992 he was running third in the polls behind Bush and Ross Perot, he survived both the revelation that he had dodged the draft and what a member of his campaign team had unforgettably dubbed "bimbo eruptions" and gone on to win the presidency.

To underestimate such a politician is a serious error, and it is, I am afraid, an error we committed in 1995–96. The test was whether we could force Clinton to sign a budget agreement by refusing to pass bills that did not contain our reforms. Well, we went head-to-head with him over the budget and lost. In November, we sent him a stopgap spending bill that froze Medicare premiums at their current level, and he vetoed it on the grounds that it would hurt senior citizens. We sent a new bill without the Medicare provision but with a statutory commitment to a balanced budget. He signed it, ending the first of two government shutdowns. The commitment was later ignored.

We passed a bill funding the Department of the Interior, and he vetoed it, closing the national parks. Likewise, he vetoed bills covering the Departments of Health and Human Services, State, Justice, Labor, and Education, among others. It should have been obvious to us that the Democrats had polling information reassuring them that the public favored their rhetoric in this fight, but it wasn't. We not only lost the battle over the legislation itself, but the far more important one for the public's understanding and approval of what we were trying to do. The second shutdown, which stretched for three weeks over the 1995 Christmas holidays, seared into the public's mind a deeply negative impression of our efforts.

To some extent our miscalculation had been based on twelve years of what had been to us a very bitter experience. We

Republican members of Congress had again and again through the Reagan-Bush years seen our Republican presidents cave in to the congressional Democrats. Again and again we had been told that the White House would simply not be able to bear the pressure of standing firm against Congress and risking a government shutdown by vetoing the budget and being left without the continuing resolutions necessary to keep the government funded without a budget.

So we did have grounds for believing that we would win a showdown with the executive. Unlike Reagan and Bush, however, Clinton figured, rightly, that in this case he would be able to win public support. For one thing, people tend to be suspicious of government irregularities they do not understand, and for another, unlike Reagan and Bush, he would have the press on his side. However much they enjoyed keeping his various scandals alive, when it came to policy, the media were bound to be with him, and that and steady nerves would make the difference.

Now, Republicans are with good reason highly distrustful of the media. They do not believe that they are likely to get a fair shake from most reporters. We know all this better than anyone, and yet there we were, designing a strategy that required the media to communicate clearly our view of what we were trying to do and what was at stake.

We thought, in other words, that issues like balancing the budget, cutting taxes, and generally changing the direction of government would be the story. Just as the voters' having sent a majority of us to Congress for the first time in forty years had for a time been the story.

When the negotiations with Clinton broke down and he vetoed the budget, the story was instead about such hardships as the families of government workers who might not be able to celebrate Christmas or the small businesses on the edges of the national parks that were going broke because the parks had to remain closed. In other words, the story about the shutdown was once again—as with the old story of the famous Reagan spending cuts that happened not to be cuts at all—the story of Republican heartlessness.

Another thing in Clinton's favor was his unparalleled capacity to fashion simple, convincing statements for public consumption that worked very well as public relations. I would watch with amazement as the President explained to a nationwide audience that he wanted to keep the government open while he was vetoing the very bills that would have done so.

I cannot understand how we ever imagined that the media would police the President's utterances. Still, looking back on that time, it seems to me now that to some extent the way they covered that particular conflict between us and the President was legitimate. It is true that they generally gave Clinton and the Democrats the benefit of the doubt. It is true that there were many, many slanted stories that played up various victims of Republican so-called stubbornness. Still, we had for a year been the dominant force in American politics. We had been on the offense, and we had been prepared to go head-to-head with the President. We and not Clinton had picked this fight, and we and not Clinton had gotten bloodied by it. Despite our having been misled by the experiences of Reagan and Bush, basically we had only ourselves to blame.

And if our expectations about how the press would respond were beyond naïve, what is there to say about our failure to take the proper measure of the massive advertising campaign, coordinated among the President and Vice President, the Democrats in Congress, and the labor movement, which was focused on mobilizing public opinion against us. Dick Morris wrote later that they designed this campaign purposely to go unnoticed by the national media by keeping the ads out of Washington, New York, and Los Angeles. It seems that as far as the major national media are concerned, if it doesn't happen in any of these three places, it's nothing they need to know about.

The White House began to design the campaign in June 1995, coincidental, as you may remember, with Clinton's decision to move to the right. He had brought Dick Morris into the White House, as he had earlier in his career brought him into the Arkansas State House, to lift his failing administration and position him to get reelected in 1996. Morris set about helping him do this with, as we would come more and more to see, great shrewdness. And, as the world to both its surprise and astonishment would later discover, by means of certain exceptionally effective techniques for raising the funds necessary for the purpose.

Clinton's advertising campaign, as planned, went largely unnoticed by the national media (might they have begun to ask where the money was coming from?). But we members of the House knew about it almost as soon as it began, in September 1995. Because we go home regularly, and have staffs back home that keep track of things for us when we are in Washington, we know of things that do not necessarily make their way into the Washington Post. I myself first came across these ads in Biloxi, Mississippi, and could see how well made and effective—and dishonest—they were.

But while we noticed the campaign, we did not properly think through its implications for us. We were committed to the idea of Clinton as a weak President who would ultimately feel required to sign an agreement with us for a balanced budget with tax cuts, and we failed to see the advantageous position he was moving himself into. The ads began in September, and in October we had a discussion with Haley Barbour, chairman of the Republican National Committee, about whether it would be advisable for us to respond to them. We decided that if the Democrats went on spending at this rate so early in the election cycle, they would bankrupt themselves. How right we were—and how wrong.

Haley Barbour understood the situation far better than the rest of us. For six weeks he tried to persuade us that our strategy was wrong. We were not going to get a budget agreement, he said, and every time we met with Clinton to negotiate, we were only strengthening his position. Haley would have had us cut off negotiations by late November, never meet at the White House, and never close down the government. He believed that a sharp and clear distance between us and the White House was clearly to our advantage; any time we demonstrated our willingness to negotiate with the President we merely added to his stature and brought ourselves no closer to any agreement.

Haley of course turned out to be right. The longer negotiations went on, the stronger Clinton became. All he had to do was repeat his mantra about how his balanced budget would save Medicare, Medicaid, education, and the environment, while the Republicans meant to pay for their tax cuts out of the hides of the elderly. I became a particular object of attention in those 80,000 negative commercials.

Perhaps I should have been flattered. The problem was that this mighty—not to mention questionably funded—ad campaign, combined with the way we somehow let ourselves get stuck with the onus for the government's being shut down, cost us a lot. It made things difficult for many of us, but especially for me—and in a different way for Bob Dole, who was required by both a highly developed sense of honor and the politics of his party to stick it out with us House conservatives. He was a presidential candidate forced to negotiate with his rival only eleven months before the election. Moreover, the difficult and delicate maneuvering that would have been natural between any incumbent President and his chief rival became all the more difficult and delicate in this case because Dole had to deal with two extra problems. The first was the force and passion of the House freshman class of 1994, who were not so much politicians as dedicated reformers full of moral certainty. Within nine months they were already frustrated at having their hopes for a militant conservatism dampened by the Senate. The second was the threat that a serious and effective opposition would be mounted against him in the primaries. For his part, then, he was better off with our having reached no agreement with Clinton, which would not only have assuaged the members of the class of 1994 but given him the opportunity to beat Clinton on very basic and principled issues. Still, he loyally stuck it out with us to what would be for him the bitterest end.

Another senior leader, however, disagreed with Haley Barbour. Trent Lott, who was then Senate whip and was soon slated to take Bob Dole's place as majority leader, believed and still believes that a real opportunity to close a deal had been at hand, but no one in the room possessed the negotiating skills to get it settled. In his view there is a real art to getting the two parties to a negotiation to concede enough so that both can get to "yes."

Maybe so. Certainly in 1997 with Erskine Bowles, Clinton's recently appointed chief of staff, and Trent Lott as majority leader, we had a very different dynamic between us than we had had in 1995. We were quickly able to come to an understanding. In 1995 the White House was represented by Leon Panetta, the

former California congressman who had helped to create many
of the very government programs we were trying either to
reform, to reduce in size, or to dismantle altogether. Then there
was Al Gore, who visibly suffered great pain at our attempting to
make even the slightest move against any of the liberals' programs. The combination of Panetta and Gore was like a brick
wall. Erskine Bowles, on the other hand, was a successful busi-
nessman from North Carolina who had had a career of being a
serious and effective negotiator.

And for his part, Trent Lott in 1997 as majority leader was in
an entirely different strategic position from that of his predeces-
sor Bob Dole in 1995. He was coleader of a congressional party
victorious in 1996 even if scarred by a fourteen-month scurrilous
ad campaign and shaken by the reelection of Clinton, who only
a year before had seemed hopelessly mired in failure and scandal. That President, now secure, stopped worrying about his left
flank and was now intent on enjoying a successful and popular
second term by balancing the budget and keeping his campaign
pledge to cut taxes. Dole had been a presidential candidate
forced to negotiate with his rival; Lott was a legislative leader at
the beginning of a new presidential term who was virtually
guaranteed his majority through the year 2000.

When we were finally able to reach an agreement, in 1997,
we got $600 billion in entitlement reforms, medical savings
accounts that both save Medicare and increase choice for senior
citizens, and tax cuts that include a child tax credit and cuts in
both the capital gains and death taxes. Still—I understand that it
was to be expected—conservative pundits and columnists immediately attacked the agreement for not being conservative
enough. So Bob Dole's fears about reaching a settlement for
1996—especially with the freshmen remaining militant and

Steve Forbes running a self-financed campaign of attacks against him from the right in the Iowa and New Hampshire primary campaigns—were well founded and justified.

In the end, then, our seeking an agreement with Clinton in 1995 was from just about every point of view a fiasco, and for my failure to have reexamined my assumptions, I bear the primary responsibility. It cost us damage in public approval that would take most of 1996 and the successful negotiations of 1997 to overcome.

CHAPTER 5

DON'T UNDERESTIMATE THE LIBERALS

SOMETIMES EVEN VERY experienced people can be utterly naïve. When we conservatives won the election of 1994, we fancied that the whole Washington power structure was about to change. During the campaign season we had talked ourselves into believing that winning the 1994 elections would be just about all it would take to turn things around. There is no question that some very important shift in the political and cultural tectonic plates had been taking place in the country out there. Otherwise, why, for instance, would Clinton have found it advisable, under the tutelage of Dick Morris, to position himself considerably to the right of where he had spent the early days of his presidency? But it takes a whole lot more than an election—or even two or three—for power elites to give up.

We of all people should have understood that. Had we not ourselves endured forty years of defeat without giving up our convictions? We had survived not only ordinary defeats but even crushing landslides like those of 1964 and 1974 without letting go of any of our positions. After Watergate, in the House we had found ourselves a minority of 144 to the Democrats' 291, and yet we had not surrendered a single notion or ambition.

Yet here we were in 1994, with one victory under our belt and a relatively modest 230 to 205 majority, lulling ourselves into the expectation that the liberal elites would decide they had to accept the judgment of the American people and adjust both their beliefs and their programs accordingly.

The liberals, of course, had an entirely different view of what had happened. They viewed us simply as accidental inter-lopers who had somehow usurped what belonged to them by right. They had no thought of being accommodating. Quite the opposite. In their view they had to attack us, assault us, and drive us from power by any and all possible means, and in the shortest time possible.

The truth is, this was a perfectly understandable and even a legitimate response for liberals who had been the governing elite for over sixty years and who had actually controlled the House for sixty of the last sixty-four years. Why would anyone expect them not to do everything necessary to take back power? Nor did we on our part do anything to mitigate their determination. On the contrary, we both spoke and behaved as if there were lit-tle ground on which to build any kind of bipartisan cooperation. Sam Rayburn had famously said that to get along you had to go along. But we were in no mood either to get along or to go along. Rayburn's principle worked only when people agreed on the basic things—as Democrats did, for example, in enacting the New Deal—but could not apply in the case of real ideological difference.

The tone we would take was set during the wee hours of election night 1994 in the course of a planning discussion in Georgia. About forty of my closest allies and supporters, together with my family, were sitting together for a rehash of our victory, and we were, as you can imagine, all very elated. As we were talking about what we would do as the controlling party in Congress, John Uhlmann, an old friend and supporter from Kansas City, turned to me and said, "Please don't go to Washington and grow." I couldn't figure out what he meant; surely he expected me to learn a thing or two I hadn't known before in the office of the Speaker.

"What do you mean?" I asked him.

John said, "I have been involved in campaigns for years, and every time we help to get someone elected who shares our view of the world and our political beliefs, we send him or her off to Washington with high hopes. At first he sticks to his guns, then gradually he begins to be absorbed into the Washington establishment, and before you know it, there are articles in the press about how much he has 'grown.' In Washington, 'growing' means moving to the left. That's after all where the elite people are. I myself prefer conservatives who never grow."

That was early Wednesday morning. On Friday I had my first public appearance in Washington as Speaker-elect. It was in the Willard Hotel, and I will never forget the crush of cameras and reporters jammed in the hallway as I tried to get into the room to make my speech. I tried then to formulate for myself John Uhlmann's caution. "We will cooperate but we will not compromise," I said. "We will work with the Clinton Administration when we can find common values and common ground. We will not, however, compromise our principles or abandon our agenda simply for the sake of working together."

I have ever since tried to adhere to that position. In Washington, it's not exactly the way to win a popularity contest.

If you are not a philosophically committed conservative, it might be difficult to understand the fear of Washington that is a key part of the conservative experience. Since 1932 conservatives have been struggling with an increasingly liberal Democratic Party. Most conservatives are driven by a distrust both of government and of ideas that undermine what they know to be American values. For most of the more than sixty years since Franklin Delano Roosevelt came to power they have felt their ideas and way of life to be under increasing pressure. Abroad, of course, there was the threat of totalitarianism in the various forms called Nazism, fascism, and Communism. At home, they felt their freedom threatened by larger and larger and more and more intrusive bureaucracies. They saw their values being scorned and trampled by the education system, especially the universities, and by the entertainment industry. They saw their very contact with reality under assault by the liberal news media. They also saw enormous power being wielded by a handful of Washington labor bosses who exacted vast sums of money from their union members to be used politically in ways those members had no say in. They have been witnessing the metastatic growth of the number of predatory trial lawyers, who have brilliantly figured out how to shake down American industry mercilessly and stay protected by the Democratic Party.

In addition, they have had a long and bitter experience—the experience John Uhlmann was warning me about—of electing candidates who quickly melted into the Washington establishment. They had not had consistent victories or reliable leaders since the 1920s. Even Ronald Reagan, our greatest and most beloved modern leader, worked with moderates. He had cut deals with the Democratic Congress, and they blocked him from cutting back on the size of government.

In fact, the mixed experience of the Reagan Administration is a good example of the power of the liberal elite. Even as shrewd a communicator as Reagan had to pick his fights very carefully and to limit the number of things he could fight for. His subordinates found early on that despite their boss's enormous popularity and skill with the press, they could not defeat the Democratic congressional establishment except on the biggest and most visible issues.

The Reaganites who remained true to the conservative legacy found themselves being dragged through the mud by the press, among other things finding damaging information about themselves leaked to both the political columnists and the gossip columnists. On the other hand, Republicans who were willing to compromise the values of their party were described as "courageous," "innovative," and "thoughtful."

If a conservative was invited to the "right" Georgetown cocktail parties, he would almost immediately find himself engaged in some heated argument (in which case he would very likely not be invited again), or he would listen politely to the liberal chat that was invariably the staple of any high-fashion Washington party. In the latter case, he would either hate himself for being a coward or begin little by little to believe that the liberals were not all that wrong about things. This process is not unique to Washington, but in Washington it can be of great consequence to the country.

So it was that when we became the majority, we steeled ourselves against the kind of bipartisanship that might in any way cost us our convictions. One reason we had given ourselves a time limit of only one hundred days to pass the Contract With America was that we were determined not to get drawn into playing any kind of game with the Democrats. True, our majority was narrow, though after five Democrats came over to us and we won a special election, it widened, but we began with 230 votes, and in the House 218 is the decisive number.

Had we been traditional Republicans, we might have arrived in Washington as so many had done before us, sat down with the Democrats and the Clinton Administration, and sought to govern in a bipartisan spirit. That way we would have been far more acceptable, received far better press, and paid a far smaller price. We would also have changed things a whole lot less and been a bitter disappointment to our grassroots supporters.

Therefore, in January 1995, when we were all sworn in, to be accommodating to our political opponents was simply not a possibility. Our freshman class was a group of idealists who were truly outraged by the Clinton tax increase, by Clinton's proposal for nationalized health care, and by the Democrats' whole package of liberal social policies in welfare, quotas, set-asides, and so on. As for the leadership, we were bonded together by the experience of drawing up the Contract With America and our mutual pledge to do everything in our power to see that it passed. We were riding the tide of history. How could we engage in the same kind of betrayal we had once so bitterly condemned in other Republicans?

In retrospect I still think we were right to follow the path of no compromise, but we should have realized and prepared ourselves for the consequence of doing so. Unfortunately, we were under the illusion that the Democrats would be forced to give in to us because of pressure from the public. Hadn't our victory proven what a lot of us had known in our bones for some time: that our ideas were growing ever more popular with the American people? We were right about this! I have never doubted it. But we failed to take into account both the Democrats' ability by means of rhetoric to fake support for something they opposed and the passion of their party's political base to see us defeated in every possible way.

Early in 1995, right at the beginning of our majority, Senator Paul Coverdell cautioned me, "We have not won the war, we are simply on the beach at Normandy and now we have to fight our way through the hedgerows and across Europe. The Left is not about to ask for an armistice or negotiate their own surrender. They are going to do everything they can to throw us back into the minority and end our threat to their values and their power structure."

Deep down I recognized the truth of what Paul was saying. I expected the liberals to fight us. But the depth of my conviction that they would fiercely try to oppose us was not matched by an equal depth of planning for what to do about it. To be realistic, perhaps it is impossible, or in any case unproductive, to spend too much time worrying about what your opponent is going to do. Nevertheless, the difference between the well-thought-out, unending, and no-holds-barred hostility of the left and the acquiescent, friendship-seeking nature of many of my Republican colleagues never ceases to amaze me. They hit us. We make an excuse. We offer a helping hand. They bite the hand. We offer an excuse. You really have to have been inside some of our struggles to appreciate the radical difference between the systematic hostility of the Left and the confused efforts at accommodation and compromise on the part of certain Republicans.

As I have said, joining us was an eye-opener to the former Democrats who came to serve in the Republican House Conference. In the Democratic Caucus, they said, people were expected to toe the liberal line or keep their mouths shut. They were routinely and openly threatened with reprisals. President Clinton himself came up against this kind of bullying from the liberals when he asked Congress for "fast track" legislation that would give him the authority to negotiate trade agreements with foreign governments. One after another, Democrats said to him in effect "I agree that this legislation is good for the country, but the union leadership would kill me." Or, as one of them said, "For me this is a $200,000 decision, because if I vote for fast track the union leaders will run someone against me in the primary and cut off my contributions." This member would be in fact under a double threat, because in addition to having the power to run someone in a primary against him, the unions provide the Democrats with half of all their PAC (political action committee) money, so his sources of funding would dry up. Another man was told, "We may not be able to beat you in your own district, but if you should ever run for statewide office, we will run someone against you." And when Clinton remarked in public that he believed fast track legislation would pass handily if there could be a secret vote, he absolutely enraged those liberals for whom coercion is key to their mode of operation.

The media have in recent years become fixated on the questions of corporate contributions and what they call "soft" money for financing campaigns, but the truth is, nothing on the right is at all comparable to what the unions do. First of all, corporations are much less capable of being organized—each of them operates politically on its own—and they are, as profit-seeking institutions, much more inclined to seek accommodation with whoever is in power. Labor bosses, on the other hand, have a strategic view of politics and spend a great deal of time and effort developing long-term political muscle. By contrast corporate leaders focus mainly on their respective businesses and spend very little time or effort on politics. When major business leaders do for one reason or another concern themselves with Washington, they usually set up Washington offices or hire lobbyists and leave matters to them. Now, many if not most people who leave high-level government jobs in Washington seem to stick around looking for work as lobbyists. And when you consider that Congress was controlled by the Democrats for sixty of the last sixty-four years, it makes perfect sense that the majority of corporate representatives in Washington should turn out to have been Democratic staffers. Thus in 1996, for example, a number of the people serving as advisers to corporations spent the last weeks of the campaign advising their bosses to give money to the Democrats in case they should be returned to power. A rational business strategy, of course, would dictate their going all out to ensure a Republican victory. Just think, for instance, of a House Ways and Means Committee chaired by Charlie Rangel instead of Bill Archer, or a House Commerce Committee headed by John Dingell rather than Tom Bliley. For business a liberal Democratic victory would be a disaster. Still, many of the corporate representatives in Washington were looking forward to having their old friends—in some cases, their former employers—back in power. Even now, when all the signs indicate that the Republicans are here to stay for a good while, whichever "government relations" corporate officials making decisions about whom to hire as a Washington representative still seem to favor Democrats over Republicans. Their corporate bosses by and large still go along.

I have discussed in an earlier chapter, there is another source of great Washington power: the media. Many, many years ago a young journalist named David Halberstam, who had won a Pulitzer for his reporting from Vietnam, described how the President of the United States would each morning read the *New York Times* an hour before intelligence reports reached his desk. By the time he got the scoop from military intelligence, his view of what was going on would inevitably have been framed by the content of that day's *Times*. While Halberstam might have been exaggerating (or even just bragging), there is much truth to the idea that being in Washington makes it difficult to escape from a daily pounding by the *Times* and *Post*.

But there is another great source of liberal power, not quite the same thing as the press but working hand in hand with it—in fact, usually working for it—and that is news media public opinion polls. Politicians, of course, pay great attention to the polls, as to a lesser extent do the voters. The question is, what do these polls really poll, and to what end? The pollsters, of course, will tell you that they are no more than neutral measurers of opinion, but John Morgan, possibly the best Republican student of elections in the country, thinks otherwise. He is convinced that news media public opinion polls are deliberately slanted against Republicans. In his opinion, this serves three purposes: to undermine our morale, to suppress Republican voter turnout ("We've already lost, so why go vote?"), and to cut into Republican fundraising ("They're going to lose, so why bother?").

Polls can be manipulated: through the pools selected for polling and through the wording of the questions. First of all, if you ask all adults rather than likely voters, your results will be skewed by the responses of people who are not interested in politics and will therefore be more likely simply to parrot what they have picked up from television. The more likely you are to vote, the more likely you are to pay attention to the arguments. As we've lately been discovering, the more you pay attention to the arguments, the more likely you are to vote for us. Michael Barone, an expert on opinion, says that October is nowadays the Republican month, for October is the time when Republicans have the resources to do serious advertising and get their message across. These days as soon as people begin seriously to attend to the issues, they tend to move our way. Take the case of Jim Gilmore, governor of Virginia. In early 1997 he was nineteen points behind in the polls, but he went on to win the governorship in a landslide with a clear plan to cut taxes.

So the first thing to notice about a poll is who has been polled: all adults, registered voters, or likely voters. When it comes to politics, a poll of all adults is plain nonsense and can be assumed to be skewed to the left. A poll of registered voters is somewhat more accurate and a little less skewed. Likely voters provide a poll with reasonable reliability. Even then you have to look at when it was taken and how the voter groups are weighted.

Another thing you have to look at is how the questions are asked. For instance, quotas and set-asides for groups officially designated as disadvantaged are much more unpopular than the same things when they are called affirmative action. In one recent poll people by a margin of 79 to 16 percent favored the government giving business to the one with the lowest competitive bid over a minority set-aside. Even among African Americans the vote was 48 to 44 percent against set-asides. The attitude to the phrase "affirmative action," however, was much more ambivalent. A fascinating example of this kind of ambivalence was a poll taken in the old Cold War days, when the left was advocating a nuclear freeze, that is, that the United States and the Soviet Union should both stop where they were and deploy no more weapons. In the same poll, some 68 percent of those polled said they were in favor of a nuclear freeze while 75 percent said the United States must remain number one in military superiority worldwide.

All this was very powerfully brought home to me when we were trying to negotiate a balanced budget with tax cuts. Again and again the news media polls would ask, "Do you prefer a balanced budget or tax cuts?" and again and again they would discover that if forced to choose between the two, people would choose the balanced budget. It was infuriating. We were working to get both, and any pollster who paid attention had to know that. Finally in frustration we had a Republican pollster offer the choice of a balanced budget with lower government spending and tax cuts or a balanced budget with no tax cuts but with higher government spending. That happened to be the choice that we actually offered. Not surprisingly people overwhelmingly (79 to 17 percent) chose smaller government and lower taxes.

This polling bias is only the tip of the iceberg as far as media manipulation of the political and cultural struggle now taking place in the country is concerned. It is an enormous stumbling block in our way. For, after all, we Republicans are not merely engaged these days in a traditional power struggle over who controls government. We are a movement, a group engaged in an effort to do nothing less than change the country's habits of governance so that they more truly reflect the manners and morals of the vast majority of the American people. The hostility we experience from our opponents, then, is of a far different kind from that normally felt from political competitors. It turns everything we try to do, no matter how simple and obvious, into what feels like a life-and-death struggle.

People tell me that I have a tendency to get overheated; that, especially in Washington, cooler is better. Perhaps they are right, but hear now the story of our experience in trying to balance the budget, something that, by means of whatever kind of polling was used, Americans were clearly indicating they supported. First we were told it was impossible to balance the budget. We should stick to the doable. Then when it became clear we were determined to do it, and that, moreover, the people were with us in this, we were told that balancing the budget was too important to be muddled by tax cuts. Next we were attacked for cutting government spending. This is how the liberals always characterize cutting the rate of increase. As the balanced budget with tax cuts began to take shape, we were told that the tax cuts, for which we had been attacked because they forced cuts in government spending, were now so small they were not worth the effort. Later, in the summer of 1997, when we had actually passed, and the President had actually signed into law, the first balanced budget plan since 1969 and the first tax cuts in sixteen years, we were told that balancing the budget was really inevitable because of economic growth and that we were actually slowing it down because of our tax cuts. So it went, and so it continues to go.

This constant barrage of hostility has had a good deal of impact. Because we have had to spend so much time on the defensive, because in 1996 so much money had been spent on so fierce and vicious a campaign against our candidates, and because after all we are only human, there are those among us who have been shaken. Remember: Members of Congress are required to go through the rigors of campaigning every two years. If the Republicans' experiences in 1996 are any guide, the more we win, the more enraged the liberals become. A number of our members were so shaken by the viciousness of 1996, they felt they could not go through that again. Some said they could not personally volunteer to be in another fight like the one we had with the Clinton Administration even if they believed they could win it.

In the light of our 1996 victory, no matter how hard-won, I knew that time was on our side and that as long as we worked for the American people's agenda we were going to be in power until the year 2000. Yet it was almost impossible to communicate that confidence. Most reporters, with the notable exception of Michael Barone, declared that though we had won fifty-three seats in 1994 and had five Democrats switch to Republican, our loss of nine seats in 1996 was a major catastrophe for us. The fact that we were keeping control for the first time in sixty-eight years was ignored as utterly inconsequential. You can understand, then, that it has required great discipline for us to stay focused on getting the job done while all around us the news we have heard and read has concerned itself almost exclusively with our problems.

The fact is, we had some rather spectacular victories in 1997. Rudy Giuliani won by a landslide in the New York mayoral election—even in Manhattan, heartland of the liberal elite; Dick Riordan of Los Angeles was also reelected by a landslide; Bret Schundler was the first Republican to be reelected mayor of Jersey City in this century. In fact, we won every significant race. Norman Coleman, the mayor of St. Paul, Minnesota, had switched to the Republican Party and won handily. Coleman's switch, in fact, is part of a much larger nationwide pattern in which more than 350 Democratic elected officials, including two senators and five House members, have come over to us since Clinton's 1992 election. In Georgia alone in 1997 four state representatives made the switch, and more are expected. John Morgan analyzed the phenomenon for me. "In rural and small-town America the Democrats are getting crushed."

This is a long-term trend, yet you will look long and hard to find it getting any serious press coverage or having any effect on the thinking of the elite political community in Washington. What is actually happening is that the Republicans are riding a wave of generational change. Baby boomers and their children are growing steadily more conservative and more critical of government failure to deliver goods and services in a style and to a standard comparable to those of the private sector. On their side, the Democrats are being dragged downhill by a combination of their industrial-age institutions, such as the labor unions, government bureaucrats, and trial lawyers, and their ideological base groups, such as radical feminists, homosexual activists, and race politicians. These all keep the Democratic Party committed to policies and institutions that often violate the public's sense of decency and that cannot meet their demands for a dollar's worth of government service for a dollar of taxes.

This does not apply, of course, to every single election. As history shows us, decisive elections are presaged by hundreds of seemingly small events, such as Lincoln and many others leaving the Whigs and becoming Republican, the Progressives leaving the Republican Party and after a decade sliding over into the ranks of the Democrats, and recently, southern and blue-collar Democrats moving into Reagan's Republican Party. Most of these events, which form historic trends, are barely noted in the media while they are happening, with the result that the view of the world that often dominates in Washington and New York and

Cambridge, Massachusetts, is almost 180 degrees different from the view of the world of everyday practical political leaders.

Ironically, the people who are actually most disadvantaged by this are the liberal Democrats, whose skewed sense of reality is made all the more distorted by their cheering sections in the national media.

Thus the difficulties experienced by conservatives are only tactical rather than strategic. Underlying trends may for one reason or another hit some snag but will continue, there is no doubt about that. Still, when our members are day in and day out bombarded by negative polls and news stories and "expert" political analyses (very much including many of the weekend analysts who sit in Washington TV studios and with a remarkable lack of understanding and insight pontificate about the country), they naturally tend to get upset and demand that their leaders take some corrective action.

During 1997 it took an enormous act of will to ignore all the griping and negative attacks. I freely confess that sometimes my discipline broke down and, much as I knew it was not the way to go, I would respond with hostility to the unfavorable things that were being said about me. This was of course the wrong thing to do and only had the effect both of keeping the story alive and of making me look petty. It would, on the other hand, be most interesting to see how certain members of the media would respond to the kind of treatment they regularly hand out to their unacknowledged opponents. I was perfectly confident that if we could be calm and cheerful we would automatically gain ground. If we could get an agreement to balance the budget, save Medicare, and cut taxes, we would be taking all the 1996 issues off the table, thereby both vindicating our members and inoculating them against future attacks. And if in addition we could go on just calmly picking up Democrats who were choosing to switch to us and go on winning special elections, the Democrats would be suffering debilitation no matter what happened to the President's favorability rating.

Since the Washington elites were paying no attention to the tidal pull below the surface and were instead absorbed by the surface news, they kept focusing on the alleged turmoil within the House Republican ranks (a story in itself and about which there will be more to say in a later chapter), as well as on the President's Teflon quality in the face of all the investigations of his conduct. Thus it was easy for them to believe the liberal analysts who were telling them that we had been a mere blip on the radar screen and were on our way out. The good cheer this engendered was only temporarily eclipsed by election night results in 1997, but there is no question that they keep deluding themselves.

Our troubles with the self-deceiving liberals were oddly enough compounded by the problems we were also experiencing in 1997 with certain conservative journals of opinion and editorial columns. The *Wall Street Journal* and *Washington Times* editorial pages, conservative columnists with national syndication, the *National Review,* the *Weekly Standard,* the *American Spectator, Human Events,* and certain talk-radio hosts play a significant role in the conservative movement. They provide an alternative view of events in the world, and they are collectively a mechanism for maintaining the morale of conservative activists. It is important to understand that the conservative movement itself entered the year 1997 in a very different frame of mind from that of House Republicans. Where the House Republicans were exhausted and needed a little time to think through their strategy for dealing with a reelected liberal President and to set the stage for the 1998 election, the conservative activists were spoiling for a fight and wanted to see daily or at least weekly action. And whereas most Americans, including ordinary conservatives among them, wanted to see the newly reelected President and Congress work together to achieve some further movement in the direction of changing governmental policy, conservative movement spokesmen were so passionately disapproving of this President that they were only going to be satisfied by being able to witness ongoing conflict between Capitol Hill and the White House.

There was a period in the summer of 1997 when I felt close to being disoriented. I knew from reports by my political advisers John Morgan and Joe Gaylord that we were winning in the countryside. And I knew that strategically speaking, a budget agreement largely on our terms, tax cuts largely on our terms, and saving Medicare almost entirely on our terms would almost certainly guarantee us victory in 1998. At the same time our best friends in the conservative movement press were very critical of and sometimes outright hostile to what we were trying to do, because they believed we could do more.

At that point, the only thing that helped me keep my wits about me was thinking about history. I rely heavily for this very necessary kind of exercise on a dear friend and ally Steve Hanser, who was formerly the head of the history department at West Georgia College, where I used to teach. One of the best resources for what you might call the steadying of my soul at that moment was reading James McPherson's *Battle Cry of Freedom*, a magnificent history of the Civil War. McPherson vividly describes how in 1864 Lincoln was given the cold shoulder by his erstwhile friends and allies. Reading history is naturally enriched when it bears on your own experience. Not that I equate myself with Lincoln or our ongoing struggles against the liberals with a bloody war to keep the United States from actually splitting into two sovereign nations, one free and one slave. But when you feel yourself beset, or in a period of gloom, being reminded of Abraham Lincoln at the time when no one recognized the approaching victory is not only an important lesson but a great solace as well. For about four months, then, I felt myself caught in a vise: too committed to the conservative sense of what the country needed to be able, in John Uhlmann's unforgettable phrase, "to grow in a liberal direction," and on the other hand, being hit by many of the conservative activists, who ought to have been my allies, for being too accommodationist. By the end of those four months, however, through some tough negotiation and because he was a clever enough politician to read the handwriting on the country's wall, we got the President to sign our major bills with only a few adjustments. He also believed in *our* version of "fast track" legislation, but then found he could not bring nearly enough Democrats along with him to get the bill passed into law. Perhaps above all, our members were cheered by being reminded that if we stay the course and aren't blown over by every passing wind, they will find themselves in a long, winning campaign of many years to complete implementation of our beliefs.

One of the biggest and most important lessons I have learned as Speaker is never to underestimate the tenacity of our opponents in the press, universities, the unions, and among the trial lawyers and other profiteers from the liberal worldview. The election of 1994 was a genuine trauma to the left, and they had every legitimate reason to respond accordingly (though, to be sure, some of what they did was not only illegitimate but has been attacked as being illegal). We must expect them to continue to fight us, and where they do so seriously and honestly, to respect them for it while continuing to work night and day for our success. If the conservative movement had survived LBJ and Watergate by assuring itself that values were more important than popularity, we can expect the liberals to do no less. After all, they have something tempting to promise people that we do not, namely, the quick fix and the easy buck. True, Americans are nowadays especially sick and tired of the oppressive politically correct culture that has grown up around them. But it is well to remember that temptation is something ever lurking, waiting to exploit human weakness, especially in times of sorrow and difficulty. What we have to offer people instead is strength and adventure, the experience of a new level of life-enhancing energy, and love of a great country. We have no reason to become distressed—as many members of the House did and as I at some point also did. What we are embarked on is what they call steady work, more than enough for a lifetime.

CHAPTER 6

KNOW THE DIFFERENCE BETWEEN RIGHT AND WRONG

Ethics I

I FOR ONE CERTAINLY HAVE had no call to underestimate the liberals, as, if you have not done so already, you will most certainly discover in my next chapter. But if in the 1960s you had been a young man cutting his political teeth in the state of Georgia, as I once was, probably the last thing that would have come into your mind was the image of Democratic politicians as people easily given to feelings of moral outrage—or even pretending to have such ideas.

For us young Georgia Republicans the shoe was entirely on the other foot. There were times when it felt as if we had been consigned to living in a kind of music hall world where we were the only members of the audience not laughing. For instance, Marvin Griffin had recently been the Democratic governor, and he had been positively debonair about his own corruption. At one point he was accused of having purchased for the state boats that had no bottoms. He instantly replied that the boats had been bought for those state parks that had no lakes. In those years corruption was so endemic in my state that in 1962 Griffin ran for governor again and almost won.

All this may have seemed funny, but it was not as far as I was concerned. I took corruption very seriously—not only for what it was doing to Georgia politics but for what it can do to the spirit of the whole country. My very first congressional race, in 1974, was devoted to the issue—as well it might have been. My opponent was the state's senior incumbent, John J. Flynt, Jr. Congressman Flynt had a farm, some acres of which he rented to the Ford Motor Company to serve as a parking lot for one of the company's plants. Soon after he introduced an amendment to the Clean Air Act that was most favorable to Ford. As it happened, this famous "parking lot" was forty-one miles away from the plant, with lots of empty spaces for parking in between. After I finished explaining all this to my fellow Georgians, they honored me with 48.5 percent of the vote in what was a traditionally Democratic district. This was, you remember, the year when we were just past Watergate and Gerald Ford's pardon of Nixon—not exactly an advantageous time for Republicans.

The response of the House Democratic Party to an ethics campaign against John J. Flynt was . . . to make him chairman of the Ethics Committee! They were feeling high, and they were thumbing their collective nose at those of us who cared. At the same time, of course—though perhaps they had been in power in the House for too long to remember—they were thumbing their noses at their own constituents, who don't expect their elected officials to be quite so brazen.

I won my congressional seat for the first time four years later, in 1978, and my two campaigns after I first ran against Flynt also focused on discussion of the ethics of elected officials. It was something about which I felt, and still feel, deeply. I accept that there are some people, highly decent themselves, who think that other problems should take precedence over the problem of corrupt politicians. Such people may have grown tired and resigned themselves or may perhaps be in the grip of some all-embracing ideological passion that for them takes precedence over any concern about corruption of this kind. I can understand both arguments, but both are wrong. The trustworthiness of our political leaders goes through the heart of our political culture to the very question of how much allegiance to their country can be demanded of ordinary citizens. Cynicism is corrosive of everything that our Constitution was meant to stand for and hence of our very democratic system.

I don't know if back in 1979 I expected something else of Washington than I had seen in Georgia. It sounds sort of foolish now, but probably deep down I did. As soon as I had gone through my first swearing-in I learned of a colleague in the House, Charles Diggs, who had been convicted of twenty-nine counts of stealing from his staff by demanding salary kickbacks from them to the tune of more than $70,000. He was in the process of appealing the verdict. He was, to make a long story short, a convicted felon. In our justice system, once a jury and judge have found you guilty, you are presumed to be guilty. An appeal may overturn that verdict, but until it does, you cannot be presumed innocent.

The discovery that Congressman Diggs was still casting

votes in the House seemed to me nothing short of an outrage. I began to make speeches about the indecency of permitting someone who had in fact been convicted of a crime to vote on measures affecting the welfare of ordinary Americans. Imagine, I said, allowing the vote of an honest legislator to be canceled out by the vote of a felon.

I understood the injustice of the situation, but I am not a lawyer, so I began to consult key members of the Judiciary Committee about what specifically I might, or could, or should, do in such a case. Among the people I consulted was Caldwell Butler of Roanoke, Virginia, who had earned the reputation of being a man of integrity during the Watergate hearings. I brought before the House a motion to expel Diggs. Congressman Butler agreed to speak on the floor in favor of my motion.

This had now become a serious matter. Diggs refused to commit himself to abstain from voting during the appeals process. I moved to expel him. No one had moved to expel a member in more than fifty years.

Interestingly enough, the Republican leadership was against my having brought this motion. They believed—and very much feared—that a southern Republican's being the author of a motion to expel a black Democrat would be characterized as racism. But as a Pennsylvania-born army brat who had on my very first day in office cosponsored the bill making Martin Luther King's birthday a national holiday, I was quite serene about my ability to draw a clear distinction between a felon and a nonfelon without regard to race. In fact, when it came right down to it, I don't think that in the event there was any point made about race in the coverage of this scandal. Stealing $70,000 from your staff is after all pretty indefensible.

Oddly enough, it was during this period that I first seriously came into contact with majority leader Jim Wright. He was courteous and helpful, and he agreed to allow a one-hour debate on my motion before moving to table it. He displayed a serious and professional concern for ensuring the right of a new member in a difficult situation, and what was for his own party an embarrassing one.

I guess not surprisingly, we lost a vote on a motion to table. Some months later Dan Lungren (now attorney general of California) and Bill Dannemeyer tried a second time and lost again, but this time they received a larger vote. Ultimately Diggs lost his appeal, resigned from Congress, and went to jail. The House adopted a rule that is still in effect that felons cannot vote while out on appeal. We had made some progress.

No sooner had the Diggs scandal died down than there was a new one. This one came to be known to the world as Abscam. Abscam was the name of a sting operation run by the FBI to catch corrupt members of Congress. The G-men had posed as foreigners seeking to bribe members of Congress. Several members of Congress accepted the money and were videotaped doing so. The evidence was overwhelming. For the first time in history, a House member was expelled from the House for corruption. His name was Ozzie Myers, a Democrat from Philadelphia. The videotape of Myers cursing and saying vicious and demeaning things about the Congress, including its senior Democratic leadership, helped to convince members that he deserved expulsion.

Nor were Republicans to be spared sadness and consternation of our own, because among the bribe-takers there had been one Republican, Congressman Richard Kelly of Florida. Unlike Myers, Kelly was well liked, an amiable man who never offended anyone. So our hearts were heavy about having to deal with the

Kelly case, but we were determined to set a single standard. It was agreed that he would be dropped from the House Republican Conference, though he kept his House seat to the end of the session.

While all this was going on, I was still a freshman. We were spending most of our time arguing with President Carter about taxes, inflation, government spending, and the Soviet threat, and at the same time trying to help Ronald Reagan win the presidency. When I think back about the levels of energy and determination and the risk-taking of my 1979–80 freshman term, I find I can compare it only to the freshman class of 1994.

In the very early Reagan years the issue of ethics was pretty much quiet, though there was one extremely painful episode in the House. This time the issue was not money but sex—and of the worst kind—sex that involves taking advantage of the very young. The young people in this case—there were two, a boy and a girl—were pages in the House. Pages are high school students who work in the House while we are in session, mainly running errands, and see legislation in action. Normally, being a page is a terrific opportunity for young people. Pages live in Washington under our authority, and attend high school early in the morning and come to the Capitol when they are finished. It is a rare opportunity for them, and their youthful energy and enthusiasm add a great deal to the working atmosphere in both the House and the Senate. One day it turned out that two members of the House, one a Democrat and one a Republican, had been taking sexual advantage of two pages.

The Ethics Committee heard the case and decided that the two House members should get a reprimand, the mildest possible sanction. The committee issued its report late on a Friday afternoon as the members were leaving town—a well-tried technique of the Ethics Committee. I myself happened to be staying in Washington that weekend, so I had time to think about the case on Saturday morning. Thinking about it was agonizing for me because I knew and very much liked the Republican member who was involved in this sordid business. I also knew that the leadership of both parties simply wanted to get the case over with, and as quickly as possible. Still, sexual exploitation of teenagers, particularly teenagers who had been entrusted by their parents to our care, was terribly wrong, far, far worse than a simple reprimand would suggest.

I checked with the president of the college where I had once been a professor to ask for advice. He had, he told me, fired two faculty members for similar behavior, and the issue seemed to him to involve a very simple decision, namely, whom did I regard myself as representing? If I represented business as usual in Washington, I should just roll over and ignore the whole thing. But if, as I claimed, I wanted to represent grassroots America, I had better do something about this case. My decision, then, was a simple one, though what it would require me to do was extremely distasteful, namely, to threaten to move the guilty members' expulsion. A very good friend in the House warned me, "If you do this, you had better not be living in a glass house because you are inviting a lot of stones." How right he was I would not really discover for some years, and by then the stones would be boulders.

My threat to move the guilty members' expulsion convinced our Republican leader, Bob Michel, to seek a compromise by moving for censure, the second highest form of sanction. He did not really want to. In addition to the general unpleasantness involved in doing such a thing, he happened to be a good friend of the accused Republican. Nevertheless, for the sake of the institution, he did what he knew to be his duty, as indeed he would on virtually every occasion during the sixteen years I served with him. In the end the censured Republican was defeated while the Democrat was reelected and got back his committee chairmanship. I was not certain that it made sense to have brought about such an unjust outcome, but I believed, and believe today, that the long-term health of a free society demands that we be tough about maintaining the integrity and responsibility of the people in our institutions of government.

The next major ethics issue emerged as Easter approached in 1987. Just as we left town for a Congressional recess, the Ethics Committee, as was its wont, issued a report timed for us to forget about it before we returned to Washington. This time the report concerned Banking Committee chairman Fernand St. Germain. But the *Wall Street Journal* carried a small story about it that caught my eye. The report was nearly a thousand pages long, much too long to fit the quiet nonresolution by the committee. Something seemed fishy. As soon as we got back to Washington, Congressman Bob Walker and I began to dig into the case of Chairman St. Germain. We discovered he had been carrying the credit card of a leading lobbyist. He also had been given a series of sweetheart deals by various financial institutions. In other words, the chairman of the Banking Committee was in the pocket of the very institutions that were regulated by the bills reported by his committee. Some years later would be the great savings and loan scandal, which cost the taxpayers hundreds of billions of dollars. For this St. Germain had his share of culpability, as did the House Democratic leadership, for in trying to cover up his scandal, they failed to legislate to prevent the later one.

In any case, Bob Walker and I did all we could by means of press conferences and special orders (speeches given after legislative business). But with the economy booming and Reagan's popularity, people were in too celebratory a mood to take it seriously. The full weight of the savings and loan scandal would not fall until several years later. By then St. Germain had retired.

Fatefully, the St. Germain scandal led directly to Speaker Jim Wright. I had noticed how carefully he had protected the Banking Committee chairman, and that detail was filed away somewhere in my brain. When the savings and loan scandal began to come to light in Texas, what emerged soon after was the extent to which Wright was involved in trying to help some of the failing institutions. What he appeared to be up to was something that fit in very well with what I had read in Robert Caro's biography of Lyndon Johnson about the style of Johnson's politics in Texas: cronyism and self-enrichment. But Johnson had come to politics in Texas in the very different historic era of the 1930s. Just as Spiro Agnew had discovered that the style of corruption taken perfectly for granted in 1960 Maryland would destroy him as Vice President a decade later, the habits and practices that were perfectly survivable in Texas a generation earlier would not pass the national standards of the late 1980s. After the gentle cosseting by the Democrats of their colleague who had corrupted a minor, and after their willingness basically to pass over the malfeasance of St. Germain, Jim Wright's mode of operation had become too much to put up with.

The decisive moment for me came in August 1987 when I was spending a week in the field with the U.S. Army at its training center at Fort Irwin, California. At some point in the course of this week, my hosts told me about a sergeant who had been court-martialed for stealing $800 from the kitchen fund. The question immediately came into my mind, "How can we expect our soldiers and noncommissioned officers to uphold such rigid standards of honesty with a Speaker of the House so cheerfully engaged in enriching himself?" Borrowing from Lincoln's formulation that a house divided—half-slave and half-free—cannot stand, I came to the conviction that America could not be half-corrupt and half-honest. One culture or the other would have to win.

The case against Speaker Jim Wright was the biggest test I had faced up to this point. First of all, for a back-bench Republican to take on the Speaker of the House after thirty-seven years of one-party dominance over the House required a lot of research and a lot of dedication. I talked with lawyers, reporters, staff, members who had served on the Ethics Committee, and members who had once served as prosecutors. For well over a year I made speeches about the Jim Wright case but made no move to file anything against him. After a while investigative reporters began calling me with stories, witnesses, and background material. Some of it was valuable, some worthless.

I was running a terrible risk. If I failed, I would at the very least be made to look like a fool and at the most my career itself might be ruined. I could be isolated. Even my friends would be worried about being too closely associated with me. My critics in the Republican Party would use this case as a further indication that I was a hothead and an agitator. Even if I was successful, or rather especially if I was successful, the House Democrats would be left with very bitter feelings about me. In short, I had a choice between avoiding the fight and feeling shame at my lack of integrity, or taking on the fight and making a lot of bitter enemies who would be happy to see me permanently hung out to dry. What I did is what I always do when I have a crisis of decision: I talked it over with Marianne. She told me, as she would again at an even more critical moment in my life, to do what was right. Whether we succeeded or failed was up to God, she said; whether we tried was up to us.

Maybe the loneliest day of my career was the day when Marianne and I walked hand in hand down the corridor to the Ethics Committee to file charges against the incumbent Speaker. She stood by me when it seemed no one else would. Bob Michel was quietly supportive but cautioned me again and again not to overreach but to be sure I had my facts right and to go slowly and carefully.

The rest is history. The Ethics Committee eventually brought in a Democratic attorney, Richard Phelan, to serve as independent counsel and thoroughly investigate Wright. Ultimately they found so many violations that he had no choice but to resign. The next week, Congressman Tony Coelho of California also resigned. Coelho was perhaps the best political leader in the House. His drive, intensity, and intelligence made him invaluable. It was he who in 1982 and 1984 did the most to defeat the Republican drive to win the Congress along with the presidency. In fact, it is no exaggeration to say that together, Tip O'Neill (the old Boston Irish pol) and Tony Coelho (the young technocratic whiz from California) combined to keep the House Democrats in the majority a decade longer than should have been likely.

When Wright and Coelho resigned in June 1989, the one as a result of an Ethics Committee investigation and the other to avoid an investigation, the House Democrats lost a good deal of their drive and energy. Their friends were both shaken and very much embittered by their departure.

And as was to be expected, their anger and bitterness were focused on me. The press basically all reported the same story: as one headline summed it up, "Democrats Vow to Use Their

Overpowering Majority to Drive Gingrich Out of the House."

The first strike against me had already taken place on April 11, 1989, when a close ally of Speaker Wright, Congressman Bill Alexander of Arkansas, filed a series of charges against me, a number of which also involved Marianne. I can't believe how we could have been so starry-eyed as to imagine that a press conference would succeed in dispelling all the ugly innuendo. But we thought that the charges so self-evidently belied ordinary common sense, and were so nakedly political, that they would be laughed out of court by the press. Well, the intellectual dishonesty and cynicism of the press people who attended that day were enough to have Marianne leaving the room after only fifteen minutes. There is no need to go into the detail of the ugliness we encountered that day. The press behaved as if they couldn't imagine a distinction to be made between Jim Wright's book, a set of speeches he published to sell in large blocks to lobbyists, and a real book that I had written, which was sold to the general public by a real publisher. This press conference was our first experience of the news media's style of moral equivalence being applied to us personally. So that was the way it was going to be: If the press wished it and one's enemies were willing to help the idea along, there would be no such thing as good and bad. And if the choice were to involve a conservative Republican and a liberal Democrat, it would be almost impossible to reach a judgment that exonerates the Republican while condemning the Democrat. "You're another" becomes for the news media an essential expression to cling to.

In March 1990 the committee took action on Alexander's ten charges with over four hundred items ranging from the criminal to the trivial and found they did not warrant initiating an inquiry. "Accordingly," read their decision, "the Committee dismissed the complaints." Considering the number of complaints and the completeness of vindication, being exonerated should have felt better than it did.

Marianne and I had known that the desire for vengeance against me would be one of the consequences of my success, but knowing is one thing and experiencing is another.

CHAPTER 7

DO THE RIGHT THING

Ethics II

THIS IS ONE OF THE LESSONS I wish I didn't have to write about. For while the ethics attacks launched by the Democrats certainly did not achieve their ambition of driving me from the House, they did manage to inflict a lot of pain.

The trouble is that I myself had a small but decisive share in the responsibility for that pain. My activity—at times my inactivity—did not amount to an intentional breach of ethics, but it was inexcusable.

On December 8, 1994, I signed a letter written by my lawyer without reading it carefully enough. For someone whose political opponents were hard at work on an effort to destroy him, that was an unforgivably careless thing to do. The letter was going to the House Ethics Committee. It needed to be right. I assumed my lawyer would fully research the facts before composing the letter, while he, I suppose, had decided to depend upon me for the letter's accuracy. The letter, unfortunately, contained inaccuracies upon which this whole dreadful tale turns.[1]

December 8 was a little less than a month before my assumption of the Speakership. From the day after the election in November, we had begun the massive undertaking of assuming control of the House for the first time in forty years. There were daunting administrative tasks. We were taking control of a powerful and complex organization involving thousands of employees. We had to choose chairmen for all the committees, organize the transition of staffs, hire new senior management to administer the House, and consider new rules for its operation. All of this was taking place in the glare of incredible press attention, and we had to design a press strategy to deal with the constant scrutiny that would now be ours as a majority party.

We had challenging legislative assignments as well. We had arrived in the majority with a mission, having promised the voters that we would act on every item in the Contract With America within the first hundred days. In November and December, we were completing legislative drafting, setting the assignments for each committee, and preparing a floor schedule for the non-stop pace of the first hundred days of the next year. We were also learning how to establish our new relationship with the Clinton Administration.

All of this was being accomplished with members who had

---

[1]To understand this tale you must understand that there were three letters of consequence to the Ethics Committee. On October 4, 1994, my staff prepared an accurate letter which I signed and sent to the Ethics Committee. After that, for reasons you will see, I turned the case over to a lawyer. That lawyer prepared one letter dated December 8, 1994, and another dated March 27, 1995. Both were, in part, inaccurate and incomplete.

never served in a congressional majority, and a small staff that was as inexperienced as we were. We had all gone through the campaign and then continued into the transition day after day without a break. It was exhilarating, but exhausting.

If you add to this activity the fact that the transition period was preceded by one of the most intense off-year election campaigns in history, during which I had campaigned in more than 140 congressional districts, very much including my own, at the same time that I was serving as Republican whip during our legislative sessions, you can imagine my fatigue and that of my staff. Moreover, there was so much to learn that had been kept from us all those years by the majority Democrats. For instance, would you believe that we actually discovered rooms in the Capitol that we had never heard of? The Democrats had certain hideaways and meeting rooms that they had simply blocked off the normal lists. Certain Democratic lobbyists had been given official parking spaces in the congressional garages. (We soon put a stop to that.) Above all, there were decisions, decisions, decisions, including the most difficult and delicate of all: naming the chairmen of our most critical committees, including the Rules, Appropriations, Commerce, and Judiciary committees.

On the day in question, December 8, I was spending most of the day behind closed doors with other House leaders, choosing the membership and chairmen for our most important committees. We had eliminated several committees, changed assignments for many members, and needed to place over 70 new members into their initial committee assignments. I would occasionally step out of the room to meet with staff, and then return to deliberations.

At one such break my staff handed me a series of memos and letters to be read and changed or approved. One of these was a letter to the Ethics Committee and concerned some charges leveled against me by my defeated opponent in the election that had just passed. The charges concerned a college course I had been teaching called "Renewing American Civilization." The lectures for this course—some of which, by the way, featured taped appearances by such staunch Democrats as then Georgia Secretary of State, now U.S. Senator Max Cleland, former President Jimmy Carter, and Congressman John Lewis—were taped and distributed all around the country. Basically my accuser alleged that this course was not an educational project but rather a campaign instrument. Boiling some very complicated-seeming issues down to their main import, his allegation involved the issue of campaign finance and tax law, and whether I had violated the rules laid down for them. Tax-exempt educational foundations were involved in putting the course together. If the course had been merely a new technique used in running for office, funding for it would have been strictly circumscribed by the campaign finance laws as well as by the Internal Revenue Service. The IRS regulations involving tax-exempt educational foundations allow such foundations to beat the drums to their heart's content in support of ideas and programs for achieving certain higher political ends (lower taxes, higher taxes, welfare reform, free trade, tariffs, and so on) but not to lobby for a specific piece of legislation nor endorse any candidate or participate directly in a political campaign.

Two months before I signed the December 8 letter, whose consequence I am about to relate to you, I had already sent a letter to the Ethics Committee, and the committee had indicated that my letter answered most of its questions. However, they did have additional questions about the college course which would take some time and research to answer. So on November 15, 1994, I hired a nationally known law firm to handle the response.

The firm that I retained had, and has, an excellent reputation, and I had worked with them on other issues. I relied upon them to do their job and do it thoroughly. I assumed that this would include fully researching the facts to be included in the letter from whatever source they thought was appropriate. Unfortunately, there were mistakes in the letter. The fact is that I did not even talk to the partner responsible for the December 8 letter until the day after I had signed it, and I never spoke at all to the associate who did the actual work drafting the letter.

How this could have occurred is unclear. The principal criticism of the letter is its failure to accurately reflect the involvement of GOPAC and GOPAC employees in developing and raising funds for the course. The earlier letter of October 4, prepared by my office, had reflected GOPAC's involvement. And, from the original complaint until the December 8 correspondence, GOPAC had been mentioned by name ninety-two times in correspondence to and from the committtee. In drafting the letter of December 8, however—the one that I so carelessly signed—no acknowledgment was made of this connection.

I thought the Ethics process seemed to be moving forward toward clearing me of all the charges that had been brought against me, I did not think any more about the letter or the ethics charges.

A few weeks later, my former opponent filed an amended complaint. Four months after the December 8 letter was submitted, my attorney asked me to review a 52-page letter with 31 attachments totaling an additional 235 pages. The letter had been signed by my attorney and already submitted to the Committee. Regarding that letter, my attorney had again assigned the junior associate, with the help of a more senior associate, the task of preparing my response. Unfortunately, out of the 1,131 lines in the 52-page letter there were 18 lines based on a further extension of the letter I had so carelessly signed on December 8. And those 18 lines were wrong. The attorneys indicated later to the Ethics Committee that they were not aware of any efforts to check the factual accuracy of the letter.

I don't want to imply that I am attempting to shift the ultimate responsibility for the letters to the attorneys because they didn't check the facts. I made an error, without question. If I had taken more time with the letters, they would not have contained inaccuracies. However, while I failed to pay adequate attention to the situation, I never intended to mislead the Ethics Committee.

Ultimately, the actions taken against me by the Ethics Committee in December 1996 and January 1997 were driven primarily by the inaccuracies in the letters drawn up by my lawyers. Since the letters were not accurate, I had no defense except to say a mistake had been made for which I was responsible. If I had exercised the same level of oversight with those lawyers that I was exercising on legislative issues, I would surely have caught the mistake. In short, I have learned that you can never fully delegate a matter of such legal and ethical importance.

I was not careful enough partly because I underestimated the fight I was in. Certain Democrats had targeted me, and I had handed them the means. I had come to symbolize to them a whole variety of threats. First, of course, there was my success in starting the investigation which led to Jim Wright's resignation. Next there was the resurgence of conservatism throughout the country that was seriously threatening the Democratic Party and that had cost them control in the House. I was a very handy symbol of this. Nor could they seem to stand the idea that in addition to challenging their electoral power, something that could be taken as mere politics, I had also been writing books and teaching a course designed to challenge the liberal assertion of moral authority. Finally, the Democrats were beginning to drown in their own party's ethics violations, some of which I touched upon in the previous chapter. They were desperate to find a Republican, especially a symbol of the new kind of Republicanism like me, to help balance things a little.

The truth is, our victory in November 1994 not only defeated the liberals electorally but seemed simply to have unhinged some of them. For example, Robert Wright in the December 19, 1994, TRB column of the *New Republic* magazine advised his fellow liberals that they should drop all pretense of fairness and simply beat me "to a pulp." Congressman George Miller, one of the House's leading liberals, said to the pundit Elizabeth Drew, "Newt is the nerve center and energy source. Going after him is like taking out command and control." And in February 1995 a story in the *Miami Herald* was headlined "We'll Find Some Dirt on Gingrich, Democrats Promise Party Faithful." And on and on it went. During that same month, the promise to the party faithful was fulfilled when Congresswoman Pat Schroeder of Colorado, Congressman Harry Johnston of Florida, and Congresswoman Cynthia McKinney of Georgia filed an ethics complaint against me, followed by further filings in the following month by Congressman David Bonior of Michigan.

I should perhaps have been more chilled by all this than I was at the time. On the other hand, to be chilled, even when it is realistic to be, might lead to timidity or paralysis. The truth is, you cannot let yourself become mesmerized by your opponents, even if it sometimes costs you dearly to ignore them. Still, there were times when the Democrats so overreached in their pursuit of me that anyone who paid attention would have found their claims absolutely ridiculous.

Perhaps the best illustration was the charge that I was being given free airtime for my course. Liberal Democrats had filed an ethics complaint alleging that a cable channel showing my course was the equivalent of a gift to me personally. This one I heard as I was walking through the Atlanta airport, and I broke up laughing. Members of Congress get themselves onto every television or radio show that will invite them. Weekend talk shows are positively knee-deep in members of Congress. The House and Senate both have television studios that produce tapes at taxpayer expense to provide free programming for local radio stations and local cable.

Every experienced reporter in Washington knows all this. Virtually every one of them has participated in shows with members of Congress. They know about the taxpayer-supported radio and television studios in the Rayburn Building. The news media themselves have taxpayer-supplied offices on the third floor of the Capitol. I could not imagine how they could manage to report such a charge with straight faces.

At odd moments since that time I have thought that if perhaps we had taken the time to do a full-court press on the Washington media and forced them to take a close look at the "free television" charge, it might have brought them to the point of recognizing just how cheap and shallow these attacks were. At the time, however, I was far more concerned with the legislative challenges facing our new majority. I left the response to these various attacks in the hands of my lawyer. I believed that the decency of the Ethics process would ultimately prevail, and I would be exonerated.

And as they say, the rest is history. As they had begun to do, the conservative movement and the Republican Party have continued to think about new ideas and new policies, while the House Democrats marched themselves straight into a liberal dead end in which bitter partisanship has taken the place of recognizing how sterile are the same old policies they are still pushing. And as for me, I was banged up pretty badly in an ethics fight I had known was coming but had underestimated.

That very costly decision, to focus on the big things and minimize my attention to individual attacks, has as much to do with my own nature as with a conscious choice of priorities. That's one of the reasons I was for so long rather sanguinely paying almost no attention to the ethics charges. My approach to the process of competing for power and influence had been based on four convictions. First, ethics really mattered. Second, the Democrats had a bigger system of power than the Republicans, and we could never really compete until we matched it. Third, ideas were really the key to long-term success for conservatives, Republicans, and the American people. Fourth, because I was a college professor, my teaching a course for no pay would be unquestionably legitimate.

Be that as it may, between September 7, 1994, and April 22, 1996, a total of eighty-one charges against me were filed with the Ethics Committee. Eighty of these charges did not, in the view of the committee, merit further investigation. In most of these instances the committee found nothing even a shade wrong. In a few they advised me to be more careful in drawing the line between official and unofficial staff activities. They asked me to repay $2.25 for faxes sent on an official fax machine.

If you were to rummage through old news clips featuring those eighty charges and then read what the committee found in each case, you would be absolutely astonished by the discrepancy. I was being cleared of these charges by the committee while at the same time being positively smeared by liberals and the press. You would find no sense of balance in the mainstream press coverage. The charges received far more coverage than the final conclusion that the committee found either no wrongdoing at all or something so small that it merited no further action. It's very difficult to describe the experience of finding oneself in what feels like a totally inverted universe. Eighty out of eighty-one, coming on top of an earlier ten by Bill Alexander in 1989, all of which merited no further action, would seem to add up to a campaign for political purposes. Nevertheless, the people who developed and participated in this campaign never faced any real opprobrium. I was confident we would survive all these charges.

The truth is, however, that in traditional politics there was actually no precedent for the way my allies and I were conducting ourselves. As activist House Republicans, we were developing what might be called an idea-oriented system. In March 1983, a group called the Conservative Opportunity Society (COS) began to meet for the purpose of injecting ideas into the House Republican Party. We wrote books, gave long special orders (speeches on the House floor) that were the equivalent of college lectures, crossed the country again and again giving seminars. We wrote articles and gave interviews, all focused on large ideas about governance.

Since we were in the idea business as well as the election business, we began to seek out other kinds of experts than merely political professionals. We needed alternative means of communication than just the mainstream media. A whole new opportunity arose when Governor Pete DuPont resigned as leader of GOPAC, a grass-roots organization to train candidates and activists at the local level. He asked me to succeed him and I accepted.

GOPAC undertook all kinds of educational activities, distributing tapes, creating satellite television specials with local uplinks, and in general serving as a kind of clearinghouse for conservative activists and local elected officials. We were carefully advised by our lawyer Dan Swillinger, who had formerly been on the staff of the Federal Elections Commission, about what we could and could not legally do. We were scrupulous about sticking to the rules.

We believed, and we were right, that the left had maintained its majority status by building a large network of power. Paul Weyrich was the first conservative to understand just how the left created its widespread web. In the early 1970s he had been working on the Hill and had mistakenly been invited to a liberal meeting on civil rights issues. He paid close attention to what was going on at that meeting, and what was going on was a gathering of key leaders from a wide variety of organizations coordinating their strategy on legislation, oversight, and public relations. From Weyrich's enlightenment at that meeting, you might say, grew a whole raft of conservative organizations and institutions.

In December 1989, *National Journal* featured an article written by Richard Cohen and Carol Matlack explaining in some detail that certain politicians had been using tax-exempt organizations to finance some of their activities. The names mentioned included presidential candidates Bruce Babbit, Jack Kemp, Gary Hart, Paul Simon, and Pat Robertson. The scale of the tax-deductible world as described in this piece was astonishing. Between 1980 and 1990 the number of "tax-exempts," the article reported, had grown by more than 50 percent. (Some of these groups were clearly involved in the legislative process; for instance, the liberal effort to block Judge Robert Bork from being seated on the Supreme Court—to the tune of some $15 million!—had clearly been coordinated through a number of tax-deductible organizations. And in 1988, there were 51 senators and 146 House members from both parties who were founders or officers of tax-deductible institutions.)

Thus when it came time to expand our mission by having me teach a new course, I felt that we had ample precedent for how to proceed. It seemed to me especially legitimate because, after all, I had in fact been a college teacher. It was how I made my living before I came into office. To ensure there would be no problems, I decided to teach without compensation, even though the rules clearly allowed compensation and other members had done so.

Our goal was to create an intellectually stimulating course that would reach Americans of all backgrounds, giving them both the inspiration to be more active in renewing their country and the tools to become part of that renewal. My intention was hardly secret. Indeed, I outlined the whole plan of this project, which was to be open and available to any member of either party, in a January 1993 special order on the House floor. We were also very conscious of having to be careful about the possibility of technical objections, and so we reached out to the Ethics Committee for approval before the course began and before the special orders presented the key ideas on the House floor.

Dean Tim Mescon of Kennesaw State College had heard of my interest in teaching a course, and in March 1993 he invited me to come to Kennesaw and teach jointly with him. The course was taught three times, twice at Kennesaw State and once at Reinhardt College. It was also offered by satellite at a number of other accredited institutions around the country as well as to a number of citizen groups (my favorite of these was the fire department of Rancho Cucamanga, California). I cannot tell you how exhilarating it was to be back in the classroom. Students were asking questions that were challenging in a totally different sense than those to be expected from the Washington press corps—questions about the importance of religion in American life, questions that served to deepen the level of my thinking. It sounds like a cliché but it was absolutely the truth: I was learning as much as I was teaching.

I was also having fun, as were, I hoped and believed, the people who had helped me in the development of this course: Steve Hanser, who had been the chairman of the history department at West Georgia College when I was teaching there and has been an invaluable friend; Jeff Eisenach, a brilliant free marketer who had worked at the Federal Trade Commission and then at the Office of Management and Budget, had done studies for the Heritage Foundation and Hudson Institute, had been the research director of Pete DuPont's presidential campaign, and then had become the executive director at GOPAC before leaving to create the Progress and Freedom Foundation and manage the course; and finally the very creative and energetic Nancy Desmond, a psychologist with years of experience in the field of counseling and psychology, especially with children, who managed to bring a level of intelligence and creativity to our project that had to be experienced to be understood.

Anyway, in addition to our having a great time with this course, the students seemed to be having a great time as well.

Even the very liberal *Atlanta Constitution* reported that our students liked the class. Some of the faculty at Kennesaw State, however, had different feelings. Though I was doing it without salary, they were opposed, they said, to the idea of an elected official teaching on campus. The Board of Regents had approved, as had the Chancellor of the University System, but for liberals among the faculty, free speech on campus seemed to be a right that was not to be extended to conservatives.

In addition, and fatefully, the local Democratic county chairman had entered a Freedom of Information Act request at Kennesaw State, and his documents (produced at taxpayer expense) found their way to my election opponent, Ben Jones, and to none other than the Democratic whip, David Bonior, in Washington. To make a long story short, I was compelled to find a new academic home, and did so, thanks to President Floyd Falany, at Reinhardt College in Waleska, Georgia.

In September 1994, as we neared election day in my campaign, my opponent, Ben Jones, filed an ethics complaint against me. Jones had been an actor (in *The Dukes of Hazzard*, among other shows) as well as a former member of the House with a lot of well-placed friends on the Democrat side of the aisle. He had been defeated and moved into my district as a lark, and now he was running a totally frivolous campaign. I really didn't think much about his filing, for one thing, because as a general rule the Ethics Committee refuses to be drawn into considering ethics charges by a political opponent in the middle of a political campaign. Anyway, his so-called charges were a nonsensical mishmash hardly worthy of busy people's time. But one of the reasons for silly charges is to create a nuisance for someone you don't like. It was then that I asked my administrative assistant

Annette Thompson Meeks to pull together a letter answering Jones's charges. This was the factually accurate letter to the Ethics Committee that I signed on October 4, 1994.

Thus I have come full circle to the letter of December 8, 1994, and why I had been so dangerously casual about it. Ben Jones's silly bill of complaints against me seemed to have lost whatever sting it might have had, I had a first-class lawyer to take a few petty holdover worries off my hands, and everything was now going to be smooth sailing.

But the House Democrats were experiencing the trauma of our great victory and their relegation to minority status for the first time in forty years. The first order of business in the new term for a number of my Democratic colleagues seemed to be to kill my political career. They were not going to allow ethics complaints against me simply to be dismissed. Not long after my swearing-in Bob Novak, writing in the *Washington Post*, reported, for instance, that "At a recent Washington dinner party, a prominent Democratic congressman enthusiastically discussed what he called 'The Project,' a coordinated, calculated effort that would culminate in the political destruction of Newt Gingrich." Even so, I actually didn't know the half of it, for while I knew full well what to expect from David Bonior, it wasn't clear to me, for instance, that Jim McDermott of Washington State—former chairman of the Ethics Committee and now its ranking Democratic member—would have a key role in "The Project" and would closely coordinate with Bonior.

Bonior and I happened to be old combatants. He had been close to Jim Wright. He also had been a fierce opponent of Reagan's Nicaragua policy and a supporter of the Communist Sandinistas, a position for which I had roundly excoriated him more than once, especially in the presence of assorted citizens of his state of Michigan. McDermott was different, I thought, because he was the ranking member of the Ethics Committee which had a high responsibility to judge my conduct fairly.

As early as December 1994, Bonior was calling for a special counsel to investigate me, and from that point on, the Democratic strategy would be fully revealed: Refuse any agreement; demand a special counsel; use the press, which would report any outlandish charge; and hope that the combination (along with those 80,000 Democratic advertisements going on air at the same time) would knock me out of the Speaker's seat. McDermott would go so far as to break what had always been Ethics Committee precedent by actually discussing my case with reporters.

In early December 1995 I received notification from the committee that all but one of the charges against me would be dismissed. That was the good news. The bad news was that the committee had agreed to hire a special counsel to investigate the last charge. At the instruction of the committee, the special counsel was to determine "whether a section of the tax code was violated with the Speaker's knowledge and approval." The Democrats, of course, understood that once there was a special counsel on the scene it wouldn't matter whether there was one charge or fifty: They now had an opportunity to put all the old questions and documents back on the table. They could keep the pot boiling.

I was told by three Republican friends that with a special counsel on the scene I was now in an entirely new game and I had better get myself an attorney more experienced in dealing with a prosecutor. But that was the last thing I wanted. I knew I had done nothing wrong, and I was simply going to continue dealing with the committee in a straightforward, honest way. In retrospect that may have been a mistake, but even now, after all that happened, I'm not convinced that it was. I was steadily winning rejection of the various Mickey Mouse Democratic charges, and I reasoned that at some point that would begin to have an impact on the press and the public. My staff was instructed to cooperate in every way with the special counsel.

In February 1996, we got further good news when Judge Louis Oberdorfer dismissed the case against GOPAC brought by the Federal Election Commission. This had been another outrage, in which the FEC dumped 8,000 pages of GOPAC records on the court, thus adding fuel in the form of out-of-context quotes to add to the Democratic flame. The board of GOPAC refused to buckle, for which I was very proud of them, and fought the case to full exoneration.

The sustained assault took a bizarre twist in March. *Roll Call* was handed a secret campaign strategy document spelling out an illegal finance mechanism involving GOPAC, the Congressional Campaign Committee, and me. It detailed a scheme to funnel $45 million through a tax-exempt foundation to congressional candidates. There was only one thing wrong with this document: It was a hoax and contained not one word of truth. *Roll Call* actually checked it out and sent GOPAC a copy to let it know that someone was trying to plant a lie about it.[2]

In late March 1996 we were rewarded again when the committee decided to drop a series of yet other charges that had

---

[2]In light of what we know as a result of both the Senate Report on fundraising abuses in the 1996 Presidential election and Judge Conboy's legal decision on how the Teamsters Union and Citizen Action used illegal funding schemes, and the considerations of those schemes by the Democratic National Committee and the Clinton-Gore campaign, it is amusing to contemplate how closely the model of the hoax about us resembles what our opponents actually did and considered doing.

been filed. More charges were dismissed in September.

The Democrats' desperate efforts to manipulate the process continued into early September 1996, as they leaked reports that the counsel had submitted a final report and in it had found me guilty of tax violations. The subcommittee was so offended by this rumor that in a bipartisan gesture they issued a statement that the counsel had not finished his work and no decision had been made. The committee also said it was investigating the accuracy, reliability, and completeness of the letters the lawyers had submitted on my behalf. Frankly, the committee was not clear on exactly what it had found.

Finally, in the closing days of the 1996 legislative session and the last stretch of the presidential and congressional campaigns, we heard from Porter Goss and Ben Cardin. Goss and Cardin were, respectively, the top Republican and Democrat of the Ethics Subcommittee investigating my case. They told us there were discrepancies among three letters we had submitted. They were referring to the fact that the two letters containing inaccuracies that my lawyer had prepared did not square with the accurate earlier letter my staff had prepared.

We had just completed round-the-clock negotiations with the administration on the final legislation of the Congress, and members were going home to campaign before the election. They left with my ethics case still unresolved. I was running for reelection in Georgia against a candidate who ultimately spent $3 million of his own money in an attempt to defeat me. We faced an intense campaign in the closing weeks. Liberals in the press were trumpeting a Republican defeat in the coming election and declaring me now destroyed for having lied to my colleagues.

In the midst of this tumult, there was no time or emotional space for reflection. On October 8, just a few days after we had been in Harrisburg for my parents' fiftieth wedding anniversary, we got word that my father had been diagnosed as having fatal lung cancer in an advanced stage. Marianne and I had already begun to worry about him. Now we would worry about him a lot, and perhaps even more about my mother, who had so long depended on him for support and guidance. It is hard for a woman to lose the husband who is the anchor of her life, and it is very hard for a man, no matter how old, to lose his father.

On top of it all lay the weight of politics. I continued to work with the Ethics Committee and complete the campaign. The first week in November, Republicans won reelection as a majority in the House for the first time in sixty-eight years. For me, it didn't feel like a success.

On November 10, Marianne and I drove to Harrisburg to visit my father in the hospital. He was clearly dying and was already almost completely out of touch. My mother seemed lost and my sisters were in anguish. For the first time in my life I felt out of energy.

A few days later, I went to the Ethics Committee offices in the basement of the Capitol to read the transcripts of the interviews the counsel had conducted with my lawyers, as well as with Annette Thompson Meeks and several other staff people. I was really shocked to discover how little research and investigation these lawyers had done, given that in the case of their second letter, I was charged for 140 billable hours. Yet in terms of their research, to every question put to them the answer was no.

Here are just a few highlights from one of the Ethics Committee interviews of an associate who drafted a letter:[3]

---

[3]This transcript is taken from the report of my counsel at the public hearing on January 16, 1997.

Q: Did you speak to Mr. Gingrich concerning his motivation for teaching the course?

A: I have actually never spoken with Mr. Gingrich.

Q: You never had any contact with anyone associated with Mr. Gingrich concerning the facts of this letter?

A: No.

Q: Did you look at any documents outside of the attachments to the Ben Jones complaint and the committee's letter of October 31st?

A: No. Not that I recall.

Q: And you made no contact with Kennesaw State College Foundation?

A: No.

Q: Or Kennesaw State College?

A: No.

Q: Or Reinhardt College?

A: No.

There is no need to go on. You get the point.

The subcommittee also questioned me for several hours. The members indicated that they wanted to interview other people and spend some time deliberating. I left the meeting to go off to Pennsylvania to speak at a farewell dinner for my dear friend and colleague Bob Walker, who was retiring.

There was nothing to do now but keep busy. And at last, much too late, I decided that I would hire new lawyers. I turned to two old friends, Randy Evans of Atlanta and Ed Bethune, a former member who had been practicing law in Arkansas and had now returned to Washington. Randy had been a student at West Georgia College when I taught there. Later he had interned for me. He was a brilliant debater and by now a very successful litigator. He also taught legal ethics and was an expert in legal malpractice.

On November 20, my mother's birthday, the call finally came from Harrisburg. My father had died. Others had warned me that coming to grips with the death of your father was an experience you could never really understand until you had lived through it. It would take a long time, perhaps a year, before I was able really to comprehend what my father's life had been and what it now meant for my own.

That day, Marianne and I went to the organizing conference for the next Congress in a very sober mood. Republicans were meeting to choose the candidate for Speaker, as were the minority party. This is the first step in choosing who would lead the House for the next two years. Even J. C. Watts's wonderful speech nominating me and those of John Kasich and JoAnn Emerson in seconding my nomination did not break through the sadness. Jerry Solomon asked if there were any objections to my nomination as Speaker. The room remained completely silent. It was unanimous.

On November 22, the funeral of my father took place with a full panoply of military honors and flags flying. Grief mixed with the lift of emotional patriotism.

At the end of the month we spent Thanksgiving with my two daughters, my son-in-law, and some old friends. We talked about the ethics situation and the fact that it was now entirely out of our hands. I happen to believe that our fate is always in God's hands, but this was nevertheless frightening. Nor did it help that my original lawyers, who were still involved in the case, were far from cheerful about the fact that I had brought in new ones. As for me, I was pleased to have Ed and Randy with me, but I was nevertheless jittery. The Ethics Committee had still not resolved what it wanted to do, which roughly broke down to the decision of whether I had intentionally deceived them or made a genuine mistake.

I was not worried about the question of whether I had violated tax law because the answer seemed to me so obvious. On the other hand, there was still the undeniable problem of our having filed two inaccurate and misleading documents. The special counsel was a trained prosecutor, and like any good prosecutor he wanted a conviction. In addition, the Democrats on the subcommittee would be under enormous pressure from their peers to exploit every opportunity my case offered.

After a second meeting with the subcommittee members, Marianne and I left for a trip to New York City, where I would spend two days visiting my not-so-secret passion, the American Museum of Natural History. At the same time, Randy and Ed met with the special counsel. After their meeting, Randy and Ed called and said that we should meet so that they could update me on the position of the investigative subcommittee. They sounded serious, but determined. Over four days, we spent endless hours discussing the proposals from the subcommittee, with Randy and Ed commuting to and from Washington, D.C.

One condition of the negotiations was absolute confidentiality. To my amazement, and to the credit of the investigative subcommittee and the attorneys, the negotiations remained confidential.

In some ways, we all shared the same goal. In other ways, our goals were very different. Everyone recognized the potential damage to the institution if there was a partisan political bloodbath necessitated by a contested statement of alleged violation against me. Repeatedly, I made it clear that I would not agree to any charge which was untrue. Specifically, I made it clear that I would not agree to any charge that stated or suggested that I had in any way deliberately misled the subcommittee or violated tax law.

Yet, two things did appear to be the case. First, although it would have been unheard of at the time, had I sought out and retained a general counsel to look at the totality of all of my activities and how they related to one another, some of the controversy surrounding my activities could have been avoided. In particular, I could have pointed to specific legal advice which had been provided to me reflecting that we were in compliance with all applicable tax laws. This is not to say there were not attorneys around at the time of my activities. Indeed, it seemed as though attorneys were everywhere. Nevertheless, there was no attorney representing only me as my personal counsel.

Of course, no one suggested that all of the controversy could have been avoided by such an attorney. Indeed, it is impossible to imagine that any of my activities, no matter how legitimate, could escape controversy. Yet, I did agree that legal advice would certainly have reduced the level of controversy, certainly as it related to technical compliance to complex tax laws.

Second, it was quite obvious that the December 8 and March 27 letters submitted to the committee were inaccurate. The bottom line was that the two letters were wrong and I was responsible for them. The committee had expended time and resources investigating matters addressed by the letters. Since they were my responsibility, we agreed that the costs associated with the letters were similarly my responsibility.

Eventually, there was a proposal submitted to me for my consideration. At that point, the decision squarely before me was whether to agree to a proposal that would put the matter behind me as well as the House or whether to challenge the charges. Based on their review of the evidence, Randy and Ed felt strongly that if the matter were tried, we would ultimately prevail on the issue of whether the charges constituted a violation of the House rules, much less warranted any sanction. As Randy described it, "The special counsel will have a virtually impossible time convincing members that they violate Ethics rules when they fail to hire lawyers and then should also be sanctioned for ethics violations when the lawyers they hire make mistakes."

Yet, it was clear that contesting the statement of alleged violations would embroil the House in deep controversies effectively thwarting any ability to move forward with the business of the government. I well understood the risks of agreeing to a violation of the Ethics rules based on charges such as these. I was also aware of the risk of agreeing to a sanction based on such charges to both me and fellow members. Ed, as a former member, noted that the precedent set by such a sanction could be very dangerous for members. Specifically, any suggestion that members must always hire a lawyer in order to protect themselves from such charges and ultimately be responsible for the errors of their lawyers would be very dangerous.

Ultimately an agreement was reached. It involved a reprimand which signified that I had made a mistake but not one grievous enough to cost me the Speakership. There was also the issue of reimbursement for the costs that were associated with the inaccurate letters which had been submitted.

There were some Democrats who wanted me to pay a fine. I put my foot down. I flatly refused to accept any agreement that would involve or impose a fine. There is a sharp distinction to be drawn between the principle of reimbursing the House for expenses I had been the cause of and paying a penalty. There

At age two, my parents were already divorced. My Mom and I lived with my grandmother. She instilled in me the attitude that we were without money, but we were not poor.

By the age of eight, I was a devoted animal lover. My mom loves to tell the story about the time I dove into a river to save my dog, Pride. I suspect that Pride, who was a better swimmer than I was, actually ended up saving himself, while I almost drowned.

In my early teens, I visited Verdun with my mother and Dad. There I understood, for the first time, the true cost of freedom. It changed my life forever.

At age ten, I made the local newspaper when I went to Harrisburg City Hall to urge local leaders to start a zoo. My dad wrote my mother from Korea, "Keep that boy out of the papers."

This is me with my adoptive father, Bob Gingrich, at age five—the man I called "Dad." He was a military man, who taught me the importance of freedom, duty, and fighting for what you believe in. He died on November 20, 1996, the same day I was nominated for a second term as Speaker.

Marianne and I with the President and Mrs. Bush in February 1989.

Marianne and I with two of our favorite people, President Ronald Reagan and First Lady Nancy Reagan. They came to Washington to change a nation and they ended up changing the world. *(Courtesy William Green Protography)*

In 1981, I married Marianne Ginther. At our first meeting, we just started talking and never stopped. Not only is Marianne the woman I love, she is also my best friend and closest advisor.

This photo was taken at a time when I was teaching at West Georgia College, prior to going to Congress.

Election Night 1994. Here I am, with Marianne at my side, announcing the first Republican House majority in forty years. What a moment!

(Courtesy Bill Adler)

Marianne and I with Representative Bob Barr and Senator Bob Dole in September 1994. A photo from the event hangs in my office from Senator Dole saying, "You did it!"

As always, my mom was with me on one of the most important days of my life—January 4, 1995, when I was first sworn in as Speaker. *(Copyright © P. F. Bentley)*

In September 1993, I returned to the classroom on a volunteer basis to teach a course, "Renewing American Civilization." I had earned a Ph.D. from Tulane University and worked as a college teacher for several years before entering politics.

A quiet moment with Marianne in December 1994 on the Washington subway. *(Copyright © P. F. Bentley)*

On April 7, 1995, the Contract with America was completed.
We were elated. *(Courtesy Barry Barron, Stampede Productions)*

Meeting with House Republican freshmen during the first one-hundred days
in 1995. They came to change Washington, and they did. *(Copyright © P. F. Bentley)*

In April 1995, I was honored to be named March of Dimes Georgia Citizen of the Year. Around that same time I visited the zoo with a group of children from the Spina Bifida Association. *(Courtesy Spina Bifida Association of Georgia)*

Here I am with the *T. rex* in my office at *Time* magazine's "Man of the Year" photo shoot, December 1995. *(Courtesy Gregory Heisler/Outline)*

My daughter Jackie helped raise money for Habitat for Humanity by roasting me in November 1995. It was something she seemed to enjoy a bit more than was necessary.

I celebrate Earth Day each year by taking local students to Zoo Atlanta. This was Earth Day 1996.

On May 2, 1996, Elizabeth Dole and I, with Bob Clement, talk with
Rev. Billy Graham as he prepares to receive the Congressional Gold Medal.
(Courtesy U.S. House of Representatives)

The passing of the balanced budget agreement, May 1997, with (*l to r*) John Kasich, Connie Mack, and Trent Lott. We celebrated the big event in the rotunda of the Capitol. *(Courtesy U.S. House of Representatives)*

One of my favorite activities, and something I spend a great deal of time doing, is visiting with school children. Here I am at Suwanee Elementary School in Suwanee, Georgia, in August 1996.

With my two daughters, Kathy and Jackie.

I love dinosaurs. Here I am on a dinosaur dig with my good friend Jack Horner in Bozeman, Montana, on August 27, 1997.

I joined a group of volunteers in a variety of activities on Make a Difference Day, October 25, 1997, including walking in the Race for the Cure for breast cancer and, as pictured here, working on a Habitat for Humanity house.

This picture of my daughter Kathy and me was taken at the dedication of a Habitat for Humanity house. The house was built by an amazing group of women called "Women for Newt."

I'm happiest in zoos (which is why some people think I like serving in the House of Representatives). On a visit to Zoo Atlanta in September 1997, I got to hold this baby lion. Unfortunately, they wouldn't let me take him home with me.

With Marianne and her mother, Virginia Ginther, at our home in December 1997. *(Courtesy William R. Davis Photography)*

Lady Thatcher is one of the great leaders of our era; I admire her tremendously. Marianne and I visited with her and Sir Denis in December 1997. *(Courtesy Antonia Reeve Photography)*

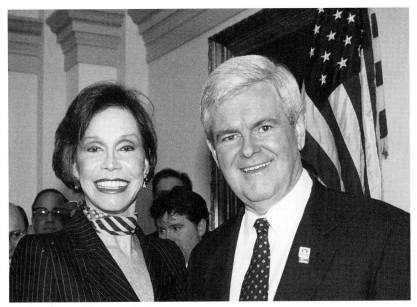

I have had the privilege of working with Mary Tyler Moore on efforts to improve the lives of people with diabetes. This photo was taken when she joined me at the State of the Union Address on January 27, 1998.
(Courtesy U.S. House of Representatives)

We recently celebrated the wedding of my youngest daughter, Jackie Sue, on January 24, 1998. *(Courtesy Warren Bond)*

was no precedent for the House to impose that kind of penalty on a member who had not abused the financial system for personal gain.

I must admit that at the outset I was disappointed, and, at times, in a rage: at myself, at my first lawyers, at the idea of having to accept a reprimand for what was an honest, albeit foolish, mistake, and at the thought that I was being criticized for needing yet another lawyer when from the very first I had been talking to lawyers and it was lawyers who prepared the letters that were my undoing. I was also in agony because I knew my liberal opponents were going to make hay with whatever agreement we reached with the Ethics Committee. The news media, as ever, would not be far behind. On the other hand, it would be impossible for me to fight the Ethics Committee and remain Speaker. Even if I could win such a fight, it would have taken five or six months of public debate to do so.

Aside from all that, I wanted to do the right thing for the House as an institution, an institution I not only belonged to but loved. Since I had for years been talking the talk where ethics was concerned, I now had an obligation to walk the walk. We had a long series of meetings in which Randy and Ed explored every option with Marianne and me, and I drew lines with them. I would not, for instance, accept the kind of hostile and aggressive language about me that the prosecutor had wanted to include in the agreement. Randy and Ed, I said, would have to see that it was eliminated. Nor would I pay a fine; I would step down as Speaker before I would do that. But I would reimburse the House. While all of this was going on, I was still in New York touring the American Museum of Natural History, which was a truly lucky circumstance because it reminded me when I most needed it that there are many happy things in life.

Then, while Randy and Ed negotiated with the subcommittee, Marianne and I drove to Harrisburg to stay with my mother. She was still too grief-stricken to contemplate what she should do now. We spent three days with her with television cameras stationed outside the house. Once we went downtown to lunch and before we finished eating, there were cameras outside the restaurant. I had agreed with the subcommittee that I would say nothing, and in any case the last people I felt like having around me those three days were members of the media. All in all, it was a grim Christmas recess.

On December 21, 1996, the investigative subcommittee issued a statement of alleged violation. Under the rules, my attorneys had not been allowed to cross-examine witnesses and, in fact, they weren't even allowed to hear the testimony. Also, the committee had no rules establishing guidelines for the admissibility and reliability of any of the documents reviewed in the investigation.

On the same day that the subcommittee issued the statement of alleged violation, I submitted an answer prepared by my attorneys admitting the violation. I did this, even though I knew that I was giving up any opportunity I had for my attorneys to cross-examine the witnesses or challenge the documents or discover any other information for my defense. I wanted to bring the process to an end as quickly as possible.

Originally, there had been numerous charges and allegations made against me. But, with the exception of the single violation contained in the statement of alleged violation, the committee had determined that all of the charges and allegations were untrue and groundless. According to the sole remaining allegation, I did not "conduct myself in a manner reflecting creditably on the House of Representatives." The Committee did not find that I violated tax law. It felt that I could have avoided public controversy had I sought and followed legal advice to ensure my activities with the nonprofit agency that transmitted and disseminated the Renewing American Civilization course complied with tax law. It also found that I, or someone on my behalf, had sent letters to the committee which contained inaccurate, incomplete, and unreliable information.

Predictably, within hours of the announcement, David Bonior accused me of criminal tax fraud, obstruction of justice, and money laundering. It was typical of Bonior to come up with the most sensational charge, however untrue, on the theory that if you repeat it often enough, people would begin to believe it.

The Republican Conference countered immediately with press conferences by Bill Paxon and Susan Molinari, the only married couple in Congress and both members of our leadership. They reiterated the truth of what the committee had found: that I had not been found in violation of tax law, that I had submitted two letters that were inaccurate, but that I had not intended to mislead the committee.

We also reached out immediately to our members. Our lawyers and I briefed the top leadership that morning, and the leadership released a statement reiterating their support of me, something for which I will always be grateful. They then began a phone tree to talk with Republican House members across the country. It was critical to give them the exact facts as reported by the Ethics Committee, to counter the outlandish statements that Bonior and others were now making.

Christmas is a slow news time, and this story dominated the media. Every major paper carried it on the front page the next morning. The Sunday morning news shows all covered it, and the story cycled through CNN virtually every half hour for three or four days. The speculation began immediately: Would Newt survive as Speaker?

At the time, Marianne and I were with her mother in Leetonia, Ohio. There were television cameras parked outside continually. The one telephone line in her mother's house was being worked overtime. There was a danger that House Republicans, already battered by the 1996 campaign and exhausted by two years of Democrats' attacks—compounded by my own mistakes—would simply decide that I was too expensive a burden for them to carry. While I could not do anything to undermine the agreement we had reached with the committee, I could make the case to members for why I should remain as Speaker.

There was a core group of leaders, led by Bill Paxon, John Linder, Dick Armey, Tom DeLay, John Boehner, and Denny Hastert, who worked the telephone tree and kept tabs on virtually every member. Every day we would hold several conference calls with this group, planning each step in the fight for the Speakership. We reached out to members with questions. We responded to the inaccuracies that were flying through the media, communicating to our members as quickly as possible.

Many members feared that another shoe was ready to drop, that further revelations might soon come out that would make supporting me politically untenable. On December 31, Porter Goss and Steve Schiff, the two Republicans who had served on the Ethics subcommittee investigating me, sent a letter to our Whip, Tom Delay, as a result of the many member inquiries they were receiving. They had lived with my case for two years and had participated in or read all the pertinent interviews. Their letter said that they could not discuss the case, which was still pending before the committee, but they could talk to anyone who would wonder how they intended to vote for Speaker on January 7. "We intend to vote for Newt Gingrich," they said, giving me my two most valuable endorsements. If the two members of the Ethics subcommittee could support me, it became a lot easier for other members to go along.

I was home in Atlanta for the ten days after Christmas, working the phone continuously but seldom stepping outside the house. There were as many as seven camera trucks parked out front every day. (One cameraman later told me that he had earned enough extra money covering me over that holiday to buy a bass boat. Every time he went fishing, he thought of me fondly.) I was honoring my commitment to not make any public statements about the details of the agreement, so there they sat day after day, bored to death. One afternoon, the stakeout grew so desperate that they filmed me silently carrying two bags of garbage out to the curbside cans and then put it on the evening news.

The press began searching for members who would vote against me, knowing that our slim majority meant that losing even a handful would bar me from becoming Speaker. Every undecided member was funneled into the media database and cited in the next story, leaving the impression of a growing problem. Members that had been confirmed by our whip organization as supporting me showed up in stories as undecided or inclined to vote no. Others reading the stories began to wonder if support for me was imploding.

On January 3, we contacted twelve members who had been listed in various stories as undecided. All of them agreed to sign a letter stating their support for me. As members began to return to Washington for the start of the new Congress, our vote count was starting to firm up, but the outcome was still in doubt.

On January 6, we had an emotional meeting of House

Republicans. The next day, at noon, the 105th Congress would convene, and its first action would be to elect its Speaker. During the conference, the members of the Ethics Committee explained how the system had been manipulated. Nancy Johnson said the committee had been poisoned by the partisan strategy that the Democrats had pursued. Steve Schiff, a former prosecutor, said the political efforts to pressure Republican members of the Ethics Committee had been the equivalent of jury tampering.

I spoke to the conference and told them how sorry I was to have brought so much trouble upon them, and I tried to answer all their questions. Some members thought I was not contrite enough. Others thought I was too contrite. A number, having reviewed the case closely, pledged their support for me. Others left with their vote the next day still unresolved in their own minds.

The following morning many were still predicting that I would be toppled. I found myself answering members' questions right up until the vote. In the end, all but nine Republicans voted for me, so that, counting two Republicans who did not vote but supported me, I had an exact majority of the full House. The fact that nine Republicans did not vote for me was an embarrassment, but after all the months of being battered, the final vote (218–9 among Republicans) was still a significant display of friendship and support from my colleagues in the House.

No sooner had that hurdle been jumped when a new complication arose. For months Jim Bunning, a member of the Ethics Committee, had been getting ever more fed up with McDermott's blatant partisanship. He had earlier threatened to resign because of McDermott and the behavior of some Democratic staff. Now he was refusing to serve on the committee in the new Congress even for the two or three weeks it would take to wrap up my ethics case. At one point he told the press that he refused to serve any longer with Jim McDermott on the committee. In another interview he said, "He has poisoned the well for that committee forever." Then just as Dick Armey was asking his fellow Texan Lamar Smith to replace Bunning on the committee (I obviously could not name anyone while my case was still being heard), there was yet a further twist, this time a truly bizarre one.

On January 10 the *New York Times* reported that a conference call among the House Republican leadership had been taped and given to them "by a Democrat Congressman hostile to Mr. Gingrich." The *Atlanta Constitution* followed suit. The story was worthy of a Carl Hiassen novel. On the previous December 21 I had been briefing the Republican leadership on the Ethics subcommittee decision. Ed Bethune was on the phone walking everyone through the ground rules for what we could and could not say about the case during my run for reelection for Speaker. As it happened, John Boehner was driving home from Florida and stopped at a Waffle House to participate in the conference call on his cell phone. In the parking lot of the Waffle House a Florida couple taped his conversation. They soon recognized the voices on the phone, and as Democratic Party activists, they felt they had a duty to turn the tape over to their congresswoman, Karen Thurman. From press accounts, it soon became clear that David Bonior's staff had been involved in discussions of what to do with the tapes. The couple who had made the tape announced on national TV that they had given it to McDermott. Evidently it had occurred to no one that taping someone else's call and disclosing the contents is a federal crime.

The call itself was more than perfectly innocent: Ed Bethune was briefing the leadership about how to obey the rules. Even portrayed in the worst light, that phone call could do us no harm. On the contrary. Four days later, McDermott announced he would step down from any further involvement in my case. The FBI announced that it was looking into the question of who had been involved in disclosing the information that was on the tape. Members of Congress, especially John Boehner, said those involved should be forced to resign from Congress.

This whole incident helped to turn the tables in the minds of the public. It was also a great help to our case for it demonstrated how partisan the ranking Democrat on the Ethics Committee, Jim McDermott, had become. At the same time the Democrats made a bizzare proposal, demanding that the final vote on what to do with my case be postponed for an indefinite period of time so that the prosecutor could finish his report and hearings be held. This was proposed after Dick Armey had given the committee a week more than it had requested to complete the report and hold hearings. Some believed this delaying tactic was to allow labor and other groups to gear up, picket Republican offices, force rejection of the recommendation of the Ethics Committee, and gain adoption of penalty that would force me to resign as Speaker. Chairman Johnson upheld the original schedule that had been agreed to by all members of the Ethics Committee. The report was then completed, the hearing held, and the vote taken as scheduled. The Democrats' manipulations made it clearer every day to everyone that they were far less interested in ethics than in their partisan agenda.

On January 21 the Ethics Committee reported to the House floor. The Republican committee members argued that it was a reasonable settlement and that it was a good precedent to reimburse the House, since it could also be applied to those who file false charges. Lamar Smith was the one Republican dissenter. He made a strong argument that the whole case was overblown and the sanction far too strong. After an hour of debate the House voted to accept the agreement, 395 ayes, 28 nos, and 5 present. Many of those who voted no were Republicans who feared the kind of precedent being set by my reimbursement and who, with Lamar Smith, felt the whole thing had been terribly overblown. Other Republicans might have voted no for the same reason, but since I supported the agreement, they accepted it as well.

Then there was the matter of how to pay the reimbursement. This was particularly important, because some of the Republican members had grown uneasy about my leadership. There was precedent for creating a legal defense fund. There was precedent for using campaign funds. Some felt strongly that I should pay out of my own pocket. Others, for obvious reasons, felt strongly that for me to pay with my own money would set a terrible precedent. We thought about it and thought about it, Marianne and I, from the ethics vote in late January until the second week in April. I needed to do something I could wholeheartedly defend, not only in the eyes of others but in my own. We talked with friends, with family, with one another. Our friends were split about this. They were wonderful and supportive, but putting them all together pointed us to no sure conclusion. Our money belonged to Marianne as much as it did to me. I had no right to commit her to something that would affect her security.

In the middle of these discussions my mother had a series of ministrokes and was taken to the hospital. I went to see her. She was already recovering, and we went outdoors to sit in the spring sunshine. Talking with her was enormously helpful. She had lost her husband of fifty years. She had moved out of her home and into an apartment, surrounded by people she did not know. She was losing most of the furniture she had worked for and saved for all her life. And here she was, sitting in a robe on a hospital bench, with pain and suffering all around her, trying to think through her life. "You just can't give up," she told me. "You have to get up every day and do the best you can. God knows what He is doing and you just have to trust in Him."

I drove back to Washington thinking all the way about what she had said to me. My problems seemed to pale by comparison with hers. She wasn't whining or complaining—what did that tell me about myself?

When I got back, Marianne and I resumed our talk marathon. She had grown up in a small town in Ohio, and in true Midwestern fashion, had a kind of solid, unswerving integrity. Her father had been the mayor of their small town, and she has a very tough-minded view of politics. She almost never does anything for short-term tactical reasons, and she is also a firmer, more patient, and more successful negotiator than I am.

On Tuesday morning, April 15, Marianne and I sat in the restaurant in the basement of the Capitol having breakfast. For two weeks, my supporters and advisers among the members had been pushing me to make a decision. I had refused to act until Marianne was comfortable about what we were doing. She was in a rage about what had happened to me and deeply resentful about the agreement and the Washington double standard, where I was being pressed to do far more than any liberal Democrat would ever have to. Finally, after all the rage and bitterness was spent, she had forced herself to look inside and decide what she really believed. Now she was looking me in the eye and saying, "If you are determined to stay in this business, then you should do the right thing. There is no point in staying here if you lose moral authority. You have to be able to live with yourself. What do you really believe we should do?"

I gulped. I was afraid that if I told her bluntly, she might get up and walk out. On the other hand, she had laid it on the line and deserved a direct answer.

I told her I thought the only honorable course was for us to pay it. If we used campaign funds or a legal defense fund, the liberals would be after me again. I knew there was a double standard, but it was a fact of life.

Marianne just looked at me for a minute and then smiled. "Okay," she said, "if that is what you honestly think is the right thing to do, then I am for it." And with that she placed virtually every penny we own in the world on the line. I was amazed— and I still am—at her calm and strength.

The nicest response came from Bob Dole. He called me from Harvard where he was making a speech and said, "I want you to know that I believe you are doing the right thing, and I am willing to lend you the money." I knew he had recently made some commercials for which he had been paid well, but it was an amazing offer for him to make. Dole has a reputation for impeccable integrity, and his endorsement of my decision would count a lot with Republicans.

So we approached the Ethics Committee about working out a schedule of payments with a line of credit from Bob Dole, if needed. One Committee staffer—I kid you not—with a straight face said that Bob Dole should certify that he was an American citizen!

We found several banks that offered the same terms on a loan, so that we could guarantee it was no sweetheart deal. Bob Dole put in escrow money he had made from his Visa commercial, so that no money from the firm he was joining would be involved. We announced that we would be personally responsible for the $300,000. Most of the Republican members were stunned, and even most Democrats refrained from making hostile comment. Marianne reached into the family funds, and we paid the first $50,000. We will pay another $100,000 in two increments during 1998, and the balance in January 1999. The ethics wars were over. The next time, if there was a next time, the Democrats would not find me unprepared or inattentive.

But I was tired. And I was about to mishandle a legislative proposal in a way that would keep the problems coming.

CHAPTER 8

LEARN TO COMMUNICATE

The Flood Relief Disaster

IT IS FASCINATING TO ME how you can learn lessons—really learn them, I mean—and yet fail to apply them in changed circumstances. That is the only way I can explain how we found ourselves in another mistake again so soon with emergency flood aid. What, after all, is less controversial—morally, spiritually, and politically—than providing relief to people whose homes and livelihoods have been washed away by a flood?

Here's what happened. In the spring of 1997 the Red River overflowed its banks, and the area of land known in song and legend as the Red River Valley was disastrously flooded. The Red River Valley stretches from North Dakota across into northern Minnesota, and both Grand Forks, North Dakota, and neighboring East Grand Forks, Minnesota, came close to being completely devastated. People lost their homes and their businesses, and there was a danger that both towns would simply be wiped out.

We were daily being apprised of the situation by various interested colleagues. A very bright and energetic new congressman from South Dakota, John Thune, had been elected freshman representative to the House leadership, and he briefed us at every meeting about what was happening. Democratic congressmen Earl Pomeroy from North Dakota and Colin Peterson from northwestern Minnesota, as well as Jim Ramstad, a Republican from Minneapolis, were also keeping us apprised of the human and financial damage that was growing greater with every passing day. And finally, we were in regular telephone contact with the governors.

Jim Ramstad came by my office one day and asked me if I would make a visit to Grand Forks. I agreed to go if the two governors and the Democratic congressmen agreed that I should. The President had been there a few days earlier and had promised the flood victims federal aid, and I wanted to make sure that my visit would be okay with everyone. They were eager for me to go.

No matter how much you know about a disaster, seeing it is a very different matter. I stood there in the Red River Valley, my eyes were really opened. Both towns were still flooded, especially in their business districts. The damage everywhere was devastating. Talking with the local leaders and citizens left me with a keen sense of how important it was, emotionally perhaps even more than economically, for a definite commitment of federal help. Otherwise there would be the danger that everyone would just pick up and move away, leaving the towns a couple of

ghost villages. I promised that I would help to expedite the sending of federal emergency money to help homeowners refinance
their mortgages and small businesses reopen their doors. The
two mayors and the business leaders expressed their relief.

A couple of days later Dick Armey, the House Republican
majority leader, visited as well. Though he represents a district
in Texas, Dick was born and bred a North Dakota boy, and he
still has relatives scattered around the state. He also happens to
be a man of deep emotion. He left North Dakota that day as
committed as I to getting some flood relief for those besieged
North Dakotans and Minnesotans.

For all our genuine commiseration and determination to
help, however, we were about to make another very big mistake.
Mistakes tend to occur when there are several converging paths
and people get confused about which is which. The supplemental appropriations bill for getting the funds to aid the Red River
flood victims came to be a very costly instance of this.

At the time, there were two other issues that Republicans
knew were of great importance to the welfare of our party. One
of these was a continuing resolution to keep the government
going, and the other was a growing controversy about developing a census for the year 2000. Each of these seemed to us to be
imperative. To complicate things a little, there was a division
between the Senate and the House: the continuing resolution
having been desperately desired by an influential group of senators, while the question of how the government would conduct
the census would determine the apportionment of House congressional districts. Unfortunately for everyone concerned, each
side of the Capitol saw the promised supplemental appropriations bill for the Red River Valley as a perfect vehicle for getting
what it wanted.

Now, the fuss over the taking of the census perhaps needs a little explanation. It has become a particularly disturbing issue for members of the House. According to our Constitution, every ten years the United States is required to take a census. To have a count of the population can be useful in a variety of ways, of course, but the reason the Constitution requires it is to apportion House seats among the states. It also decides apportionment of seats in the state legislatures, county commission and city council seats, and a number of other offices based on the distribution of the population. It is, then, a vitally important tool of democracy. The civil rights laws make the task of reapportioning seats more intricate and fraught with complications than ever. And to add to the pressure, population patterns figure in the formulas for distributing federal money. All in all, then, the census has become both a delicate instrument and a blunt weapon.

The Founding Fathers, of course, had intended that the census should be an actual count of people. The expression in the Constitution is "actual enumeration." For two hundred years, since the first census in 1790, census-takers have actually gone around knocking on doors and counting people. The Census Bureau, facing a population of some 260 million, has by now devised a system in which it is able every ten years to hire some 400,000 temporary census-takers who do just that, knock on doors and try to count everyone actually living within. Obviously, while they cannot get an absolutely perfect count, they do their best.

As it happened, the census of 1990 was very badly managed. It seems that the 1990 census had actually counted only 98.6 percent of all Americans. This is a degree of accuracy that might be considered phenomenal for a government with a 21 percent error rate in its administering of the earned income credit program and an 11 percent error rate in the IRS's handling of tax returns.

In addition, it is almost certainly those in poor neighborhoods who get undercounted. This can be an especially important problem for the big cities that depend on federal contributions to help them meet the budgets of the various mandatory social welfare programs. New York City, for example, complained bitterly about the results of the 1990 census, and some cities, like Milwaukee, went back and did a census of their own to prove that they had a bigger population than had been counted under federal auspices.

The point is, this problem is not merely one of technical interest but can have big social and political consequences. Both conservatives and liberals were eager to solve it. But while we have been looking for new ways to conduct the more accurate "actual enumeration" called for in the Constitution, the liberal Democrats had been proposing that we eliminate the present system altogether and substitute for it something they call "statistical adjustment." Under this system, the census would count only 90 percent of the people. Then with a 90 percent base, a sample would be developed in certain selected neighborhoods, and a statistical adjustment would be made to get to 100 percent. This model has been supported by the statisticians of the National Academy of Sciences as being less expensive than a full census and more accurate than an incomplete census. Dollar for dollar, they say, nationally a statistical adjustment is statistically more likely to be accurate than an incomplete full count.

The liberal Democrats were convinced that while blacks and poor immigrants were undercounted in the 1990 census, the more affluent whites were overcounted. This, then, became one of the explanations they offered themselves and others for their defeat in 1994. In their view, a census with a statistical adjustment could be worth a number of seats in the House to them.

Republicans are committed to what the Constitution says. A statistical adjustment would be unconstitutional. The Founders had created the most stable and equitable political system the world has yet witnessed, and we are loath to allow a group of statisticians to tamper with it. In addition, we are convinced that "statistical" adjustment will inevitably lead to "political" adjustment. This conviction has certainly been much validated by history. Lord Acton's remark that "power tends to corrupt and absolute power corrupts absolutely" is just as true for the census as for any other form of power. Having the power to define population as the basis both for representation and for federal funding is an enormous concentration of power. Just imagine what would happen if a small group of politicians used their own statistics to invent a "virtual America" in which it enjoyed an overwhelming amount of power along with billions in additional money: Their incentive to keep on corrupting the census adjustment process would be virtually beyond limit.

When President Clinton appointed Bill Daley to be the Secretary of Commerce and to oversee the census, it helped to crystallize all our fears. Daley is the son of former Chicago mayor Dick Daley and brother of the current Chicago mayor Richard Daley. Now, as it happens, I had worked with Bill Daley in 1993, helping to pass the North American Free Trade Agreement. He is a very solid, very smart politician and someone I very much enjoyed working with. I also admire his brother Richie, who has been a very effective mayor of one of America's greatest cities. But the specter of putting someone so closely connected to the Chicago Democratic machine in charge of the census with a statistical adjustment was too chilling even to contemplate. In Chicago, you at least had to have been alive once before you could vote as a dead man. Imagine giving the machine the power to invent virtual people while refusing to count real ones! We believe that the Founding Fathers knew exactly what they were doing when they decreed that real people should be identified in a real count.

There was one other problem with the notion of a "statistical adjustment." The idea of counting 90 percent of all Americans and adjusting the last 10 percent might in the germ-free world of a laboratory allow for the possibility of accuracy at the national level, but it would create a nightmare at the local level. The experts told us that in local neighborhoods the overcount and undercount could be as much as a 35 percent variance from reality. This is a standard problem in polling. If you have a large enough overall sample for the country, you usually have too small a sample of particular groups for any real accuracy. For example, a sample of 1,200 Americans is normally a reasonably accurate national sample. However, only 90 or so of the 1,200 will be Hispanic, and even fewer will be Asian or Jewish. These "cells," as they are called, are so small that random chance plays too big a role in who they are. A change of one or two out of 1,200 doesn't make much difference. A similar change among 60 or 90 can make a big difference.

Thus the application of "statistical adjustment" could lead to wild swings at the level of the city council, the county commission, the school board, or the state legislatures. The liberals routinely characterize the census problem as one of the whites against everyone else. But as we know, and as the liberals too should acknowledge by now, there is no such overall category as "white." Under the aegis of the statistical adjusters, inaccuracies in the local sampling might actually serve to endanger the ethnic groups that are relatively small. Imagine what could happen, for instance, in Los Angeles, where there are Cambodians, Vietnamese, various kinds of Hispanics, blacks, and "whites." A 35 percent swing in accuracy could suddenly shift power from Asians to blacks or Hispanics or from one Asian group to another, or from blacks to one or another of the groups of whites, or vice versa. Or take Chicago. In Cook County, Illinois (Chicago and some suburbs), over two hundred languages are spoken in the schools. Some of these are spoken by at most only a few hundred or a few thousand people. In an actual enumeration they would show up, but in a system of statistical adjustment they could actually disappear if the process skipped them or be dramatically enlarged if they got lucky. This is hardly the way to find out who actually lives in Cook County.

But that is just the point. If seats in the House of Representatives are apportioned among the states according to the census; and districts within the states are apportioned according to the census; and lines are drawn down to the street and block level (as they have come to be to meet the requirements of the federal civil rights acts) according to the census, we are convinced that "statistical adjustment" in the hands of politicians would overwhelm the popular will.

Now, back to the flood victims of North Dakota and Minnesota, waiting for the supplemental appropriations bill that would bring them some financial relief. Since everyone wanted this bill, and the President had promised it, the Republican members thought this would be a good opportunity to fight the census fight as well as push through a continuing resolution that would prevent the President from shutting down the government in the fall of 1997 and once again sticking us with the responsibility for it. This time we would do what past Democratic Congresses had done to Republican Presidents.

On these two issues, then, the census and the continuing resolution, we began once more to do what we had shown ourselves so adept at, namely, whipping ourselves into a do-or-die commitment. Former Speaker Tom Foley tells the story about a member of the House who took the floor to talk about some injustice. As he spoke, he grew indignant. The more he went on, the more indignant he felt, until finally he was in a rage. The more he expressed this rage and indignation, the more inflamed he got, until finally by the end of the speech, he was in a state of hysteria that made no sense to anyone who knew what he had been talking about when he started out. It would have been good if we had told ourselves Tom's story each morning at the start of business. But we didn't. Instead we fed one another's passion.

Thus it was that we devised (we thought) a way to take care of both the census problem and the continuing resolution by adding them to the supplemental appropriations bill for flood relief. In other words, we were walking ourselves, not for the first time, to the edge of a political precipice. Do or die is a heroic motto, but only if you keep bearing in mind the "die" half of it.

We were busy committing ourselves to a process we had not walked through in our minds first. Nor did we consider what would happen if the President simply vetoed our so very clever device for forcing his hand. Indeed, one of our greatest weaknesses has been to undertake things one at a time, without giving enough consideration to what comes next.

There is a reason, albeit no excuse, for this. It is a very complicated matter to deal with 228 House members and 55 Senators along with the Democrats in both bodies, the Clinton

Administration, the news media, and such outside groups as governors and grassroots organizations. The day hardly offers enough hours just for that, let alone for the kind of quiet and lengthy discussion necessary for the creation of a really effective policy, especially when it comes to handling what is a very complicated interaction with the White House. A corporation or a military command would use at least ten, and maybe as many as a hundred, times as many people to manage the number of key items that small senior staffs in the House and Senate are required to handle. Remember, we in this brand-new majority were intending not merely to serve but to overturn the entrenched liberal order. Properly executed, that would require a lot of planning.

The need to devise a proper strategy is made even more daunting by the number of key players who must be in on it. Napoleon said that one mediocre general was better than three good generals who had to work together. Imagine what Napoleon would have thought of the House of Representatives! The House Republican elected leadership meetings consist of nine members and about fifteen staff people. On the matter of the census, we brought in an additional member. For discussions on how to avoid another government shutdown, we had to add yet another member. That meant that House strategic discussions were carried on among a minimum of eleven members and eighteen to twenty-five staffers. When we moved to meetings of the full Republican leadership, about twenty-three members and forty staffers were present. If we met with the Senate there would be five to eight senators and another dozen staff members in the room. If we were discussing substance, technical staff people would be added. (Technical staff people are invariably terrific on their own subject of expertise and have very little experience and no feel whatsoever for what it takes to plan strategically in a dynamic environment.)

Again, by military and business standards, legislative hierarchies are very flat. The Speaker and the Senate Majority Leader have more authority than the senior committee chairmen, but not a whole lot more. And in addition, certain strong and willful personalities among the back-benchers have a way of making themselves heard.

Finally, the full membership of the House Republican Party—at the time, some 228 strong—are entitled to know what we are thinking about. This is not necessarily a simple affair, either. If during the House Republican Conference (usually held at 9 A.M. on Wednesdays) we brief everybody about what we believe is happening and then something changes—among the Senate, the White House, the media, and outside groups it's always possible something will change—it takes only a dab of paranoia for the members to decide we had not told them the whole truth. All these complications come into play in our planning process, and this time they allowed us to get way, way ahead of ourselves.

To begin with, in fact, we did have some leverage with the supplemental appropriations bill because one of the major things it was meant to finance was the expenses caused by keeping American forces in Bosnia. Because reimbursing the Pentagon was something the President wanted far more than the American people did, we believed this would give us some negotiating room with him. Then the floods came. We should at that moment have quickly shifted gears and realized that the supplemental appropriations bill, now needed for the flood victims, would no longer bear the weight of the things we had meant for it to carry.

It's not that we were stupid, it's that we were simply too much focused on our own intentions and not sufficiently mindful of our opponents. We wanted the census our way, but the Democrats were just as intent on having it their way. We were driven by our fear of the damage that statistical adjustment could do to the country. Of course, what we saw as a threat they saw as a hope, and they were not going to concede on something so important to them.

The same goes for the continuing resolution we wanted to add to the special appropriations bill. We recognized that President Clinton had decisively won the battle over shutting down the government. We were determined this time to take that weapon away from him. But if this had turned out to be one of the President's most potent weapons against us, why did it not seem obvious to us that he would be particularly loath to give it up?

A little further background may be helpful here. Our negotiations over the appropriations bills were going on in May, before the budget negotiations had reached their climax. President Clinton and his team were at that point genuinely afraid that we were planning to deprive them of the domestic appropriations they wanted and leave them without money for their favorite programs. They knew that if we had a continuing resolution in place, we could pass whatever deeply conservative appropriations bills we wanted, sit by calmly as the President vetoed them, and just go home while the government stayed open under a spending cap determined by last year's spending.

Somehow, for the reasons cited above, we talked ourselves into believing that the Democrats could be bluffed into acting according to our scenario. Pete Domenici, Senate Budget Committee chairman, and Bob Livingston, chairman of the House

Appropriations Committee, were both very worried and tried to make us see what a foolish idea this was. As Domenici said, "Clinton has successfully vetoed bills in the past, which includes twelve years as governor and four years as President. What on earth makes you think he will be afraid to veto this one?" Indeed Bob Livingston, to his credit, warned us over and over again (frequently in loud and angry speeches) that we were on the road to defeat and major embarrassment. He was right, of course, and we were wrong, but why couldn't we see it at the time?

The answer is that we House Republicans had gotten into the habit of trying to will things to happen. This is, I suppose, because we were always in such a surefire hurry to change the world. It is always dangerous to try to impose your will on reality, because reality has a terrible way of biting back. Whether you are trying to force an inside straight in poker, or make a bad business deal turn a big profit, or turn an impossible military situation into a victory, or force your will in an unpromising political or legislative environment, it is always salutary to be reminded that reality is vastly bigger than any man's will.

There are, to be sure, occasions when amazing things happen, when people have been known to have miraculous come-from-behind experiences. But over time, reality comes to have a weight far greater than we wish.

We House Republicans had in fact forced many things to happen. In the space of a decade we had managed to modernize the House Republican Party. In the first hundred days of our new majority we had, as promised, forced a vote on every item in the Contract With America. Over and over we had achieved far more than anyone expected. By the end of the year, however, our fortunes had quite badly reversed and Clinton's had begun to prosper. In 1996 once again we summoned our will, and despite an unbelievable avalanche of dirty-pool advertising from the labor–left–White House coalition of our opponents, we kept the House.

This time the Republican party, however weary and bruised and gun-shy some of its House members had become, would nevertheless continue to be dominated by those of us who still believed unconditionally in the power of the will. We outlasted our more sober and calculating colleagues in setting the stage for the supplemental appropriations fight.

Among our several miscalculations, in some ways the most dangerous of all, was to underrate the communications prowess of William Jefferson Clinton. Give the man a victim, and he can bring a lump to your throat and a tear to your eye. And if you add to that the opportunity to charge the Republican Congress with some villainy or other, he will positively go into overdrive. Besides that, the media usually go along with him on that particular errand. They may sometimes pick on him without mercy, but when conservatives are the opponent, they will enthusiastically volunteer to be his echo chamber.

We not only failed to institute some more rational way of reaching a decision about strategy, and compounded the difficulty by badly underestimating our opponent, we also neglected to put in place the kind of system of internal communication necessary for undertaking unprecedented initiatives.

The problem with our internal communications showed up most vividly as the debate over the flood bill reached the floor. A number of conservatives did not like the supplemental appropriations bill because they thought it was too extravagant. Many were in a heat over the impact statistical adjustment would have on the census if we didn't stop it. A number were passionate about hanging on to the continuing resolution, because they were convinced that Clinton would shut the government down again to damage us. Each of these groups held to its own agenda, and each had strong supporters within the House Republican leadership. And as the fight continued and we began once again to lose ground with the public, other voices began to emerge. Among these were senior members who thought the whole fight was foolish and just wanted to get a signable bill. They had warned us from the very beginning that what we were setting out to do would never work, and now they were becoming more and more vocal. Finally another faction began to make itself heard. These were the back-benchers who had been in favor of passing a continuing resolution because they feared the bad publicity of being stuck with responsibility for shutting down the government but who were now even more worried about the bad publicity of delaying getting aid to the desperately needy flood victims. In their own districts people were beginning to charge them with being destructive and heartless.

In short, both the leadership meetings and the House Republican conferences, to which everyone is invited and has the opportunity to speak, turned into forums for heated debates. Things were getting to the breaking point. Finally—and none too soon—I stepped in and made the decision to pass the supplemental appropriations bill with the amount the administration had requested and without means for preserving the census or the continuing resolution. I simply overruled all my associates. However, I did then go to a Republican Conference and explained that anyone whose conscience told him he should vote no would not get any pressure from me. In my determination to get the fight over with I had neglected to inform the other members of the leadership. They were so angry with me that they went to the floor and voted against the bill. It passed overwhelmingly anyway, because people were tired of the fight and just wanted out of it.

So it was that after a month of hard work and internecine conflict, we had managed to get exactly the bad press we had set out to avoid, we had failed to gain an inch on the census, and we were nowhere with respect to the continuing resolution.

In short, the flood relief bill got to be about as good an illustration of giving your enemies a free shot as any instructor could hope for.

CHAPTER 9

KEEP YOUR EYE ON THE BALL

Why a Coup Seemed Plausible

B Y MID-JUNE 1997, the House Republican Conference was tired, disoriented, and discontent. Except for the new freshmen elected in 1996, everyone felt played out. And who could blame them? They had for three years been engaged in pushing without letup, from the first announcement of the Contract With America; the 1994 election; the legislative march with the contract; the struggle over the budget and Medicare; the government shutdown; the long, long legislative session of 1996 followed by a tough election campaign; my ethics fight; and last but not least, the flood relief disaster.

Most of the Republican members were angry with the leadership for not leading more effectively and, on the other hand, angry at a number of the sophomores who from the time of their first coming into the House in 1994 had made life harder by being so aggressive and confrontational. For their part, the militant sophomores were also angry at the leadership for not putting up a tougher fight, on the one side against Clinton and on the other for conservative values. (I couldn't be too critical of these so-called militants, because theirs was a role I once played and a title I proudly wore.) And finally, my fellow leaders were angry at me for having gone off on my own with flood relief legislation and exhausted by their effort to help me survive. All in all, as the world was gleefully informed by the press, there was a lot of tension in House Republican ranks that summer of 1997.

Distracted by my own battle with the House Ethics Committee, and perhaps for that reason insensitive to how badly I had mismanaged the flood relief problem, I had failed to do what any leader is supposed to do, namely, pay attention to what people are saying, learn how they feel, and help them understand what was going on and why. I should have been sitting down with the senior leaders and the various key committee chairmen one by one and talking over their problems. I should also have been listening one by one to those frustrated and increasingly alienated sophomores.

I had completely misread the situation. Perhaps I had reason. We were on the verge of getting a budget agreement with the Clinton White House, which would virtually guarantee us another election victory in 1998 and thus at least six years of a Republican House majority. Because, as I said, I had not been listening—I thought this was such a huge step forward that it should more than offset any short-term problems we had. I was so used to being tired and battered that I tended to underestimate how much that could wear other people down. I also underestimated how just plain tired I was, and as a result how much less I was paying attention than I needed to. And because I was more satisfied on the strategic level than the immediate tactical situation warranted, I was actually pulling back to think about strategic planning when I should have been moving in exactly the opposite direction—diving in to deal with immediate problems and to rebond relationships. In short, I was thinking about long-range planning when what I should have been doing was making sure we could get through the summer of 1997. What I understand now, looking back, is that both our senior leaders and our militant sophomores had picked up on my withdrawal.

The senior leaders were a team who had really put in three hard years with me. Majority leader Dick Armey, whip Tom DeLay, conference chairman John Boehner, leadership chairman Bill Paxon, and chief deputy whip Denny Hastert were the foundation on which we had built and retained our majority. I liked them, I valued them, and I relied on them. But for some months the candor that had been so much the very foundation of our relations with one another had broken down. Together they had carried me through the ethics fight without hesitation, giving up Christmas, New Year's, and all their time off in December 1996 and January 1997 to make sure I survived. But now they feared that I had been weakened and that I was no longer listening either to them or to the members of the conference. They were getting all the members' complaints that should rightly have been coming to me.

Added to this, of course, was their feeling that I had betrayed them by my unilateral decision to end the flood relief fight, and they were if anything even more angry about my having failed to inform them in advance of what I was going to do, thus leaving them holding the bag. They were worried that this portended a new kind of unilateral decision-making without consultation, which could leave them surprised at any moment. Most of all, they resented the idea that while they were supposed to defend and protect me, I did not seem to think I had to consult, or even inform, them. To top it off, they felt they had been left to manage unhappy members without any confidence that they could get me to listen and reengage.

The militant sophomores had a totally different problem. They had come to Washington on a mission of reform, and were anxious that negotiation by negotiation, vote by vote, they were being ever more compromised. They wanted to find a way to get their party to become aggressive again, to take risks, as it had in 1995. If they could not convince their fellow Republicans to stand and fight for what they were supposed to believe in, they wanted to stand on their own and differentiate themselves from the rest of their party. They had after all not come to Washington to go along and get along—that was the aim of politicians of a different stripe. Their ambition was to leave Washington a different place from what it had been when they first arrived.

From the standpoint of the militants, things had been turning sour, and I was the one responsible. I had become a hindrance instead of a help. Some of them found the ethics fight more than they could accept. Others had come to buckle under the sheer weight of my almost wholly negative treatment by the press. Some even resented my attempts to bring people together. In short, one way and the other, I had lost their trust.

One thing these militant sophomores had lost sight of was the fact that they were only about a quarter of their own class. Thus while the senior leaders were worried and probably feeling more than a little annoyed, the vast bulk of the conference seemed to be satisfied to be working hard and going about their business. The freshmen of 1996 still had the enthusiasm of newcomers. While they too thought the flood bill had been badly handled, for them the simple experience of their first year in Congress gave them an optimism which overshadowed any problem. Most senior members (including, by the way, most of the sophomores) were hard at work going about their business. Many of them had a committee or a subcommittee chairmanship or a major assignment on a really exciting committee. They had hearings to hold, important legislation to work on, bills to mark up. While it had turned out to be harder work than they anticipated and sometimes more painful than they liked, they were still thrilled to be in the majority. Since they found the opportunities of the majority so much greater than the problems of the minority, they were willing to stick with me. So as the tension that the press was so happy to report on was beginning to build and contacts between the militants and some of the senior leaders were quietly intensifying, the 160 to 170 other Republican members were busy minding their own—and the nation's—business.

In the end, a small group of militants began to make secret visits to the senior leaders and grimly presented them with a radical plan of action against me. They were so tired of what they saw as my failures that they were prepared to gamble. They knew that they could never unseat me in the Republican Conference. It would have taken 115 votes out of 228, and they could never, under any plausible circumstance, count on more than 25 to 40. If, however, they brought it to a vote in the House, where Republicans had only a 228 to 207 majority, it might be possible. For then all it would take was 11 Republicans to vote to vacate the speakership and force a new election as Speaker. They believed all 207 of the Democratic votes would solidly join them in creating chaos by toppling me. But replacing me with Dick Gephardt could hardly be the outcome that conservative militants had in mind: It was too crazy even to contemplate.

Because I had allowed distance to grow between me and the leadership, they did not feel comfortable about sitting down and sharing their concerns with me. They felt they had to deal with this problem themselves, and they were worried. What if the conference grew more dissatisfied, and the militant members grew in number or acted suddenly out of desperation? What could they do then?

They decided it would be best to understand just what the militants were planning to do. So they met with them and listened carefully, hoping to avoid some kind of catastrophe. Unfortunately, each and every time the senior leaders listened, the militants became ever more convinced that they were being agreed with.

So yet another crisis was developing, with the press rumor mill, of course, in full flood. In early July, over a four- or five-day period, things came to a head. But trying to ascertain exactly who said what and to whom, as Congressman Greg Ganske would later point out, was like watching the Japanese movie *Rashomon*, in which each character describes exactly the same incident in an entirely different way.

The militants had threatened to make a motion on the floor to vacate the Speaker's chair. This, of course, was the scenario described above. They were, and are, very far from stupid people. They could not have meant it. In retrospect it seemed clear that they only wanted to cause a big enough stir to get some action on their grievances and thereby bring about a big change in our mode of operation.

Something like this had actually happened in 1910. The Republican Speaker of the House was Joe Cannon. On one occasion George Norris, a Republican from Nebraska, moved to defeat a ruling of the chair, which under the rules was an explicit motion of no confidence. A sufficient number of progressive Republicans joined with the Democrats to carry Norris's motion. Cannon then offered to resign. At a subsequent meeting of the Republican Conference, those who had participated in the vote of no confidence said, "We don't want you to resign. We want you to be Speaker. But we must change the rules. You can no longer be a dictator." He agreed to give power back to the House at large.

Thus was born a system of committee chairmanships designed to exercise a certain mediating power. They also created a discharge petition process, which is a way of getting bills out of committee even if the Speaker doesn't want to schedule them. Thus, much of the practice of the modern House grew out of that rebellion undertaken to get the Speaker's attention. Though of course the situation was entirely different, our modern militants were hoping that the boldness of their threat would bring about a change of the situation without any of the possible harmful consequences.

As for the leaders who were meeting with them and causing them to harbor the illusion of support, they were so evidently trying to communicate sympathy for the frustrations driving the militants, while trying to make them understand that this proposed action would be at the least hurting the House GOP and at the most committing outright political treason.

On July 10, at the end of his first meeting with some of the militants, Dick Armey asked his top assistant to brief Arne Christenson, my chief of staff. He knew we had a real problem, and he wanted me to know it. Until that moment, I had been shrugging off various press reports about the plot against me. I remembered how Bob Michel had been entrenched as minority leader. No matter how often we militants griped, we knew and respected the fact that he had a solid majority of the House Republican Conference on his side. As for what was happening now, I also knew that ten members griping was a very, very great distance from 115 members voting to nominate a new Speaker in midterm. In other words, I did not sufficiently appreciate what was going on.

I had left out of my calculations the role of the news media. The Capitol is now intensely covered, daily by *Congressional Quarterly* and *National Journal* and several times a week by the newspapers *Roll Call* and *The Hill*. Then there are CNN, Fox, and MSNBC, and a host of other outlets. Thanks in part to our very success in shifting the initiative from the executive branch to the legislative branch, we had made Congress much more worth covering.

Certain liberal columnists had been convinced for a long time that I could not last. They had regularly predicted my demise. Now certain conservative journalists were following suit, taking a cue from the militant sophomores with whom they spoke. Finally, there were enough reporters talking to one another and to the complaining members to create a kind of bandwagon for a coup.

People began to ask me about it, and whenever they did, I would laugh and say, "Yes, there can be a plot. No, there won't be a coup." This was, of course, exactly what happened. But meanwhile it had grown into a big story, and as everybody knows, when a story gets a big enough play in the media, it takes on a reality of its own.

On Friday morning, July 11, I met with the senior leadership to see if I could find out what the militants were really up to. Some of the leaders had had a meeting with them the night before that lasted until 1 A.M. After that some of the leaders had talked until about 3 A.M. They had grown genuinely concerned that the House Republican Party was about to tear itself apart.

As these leaders met with me the next morning, everyone said they would support me, but not everyone was convinced the militants could be stopped. I suddenly remembered a piece of advice given me by Bob Michel: There are times when leadership means leading. You just think it through and do it without tying yourself into knots about every possible twist and turn.

So then and there I explained that there was no circumstance in which I would even consider stepping down. I was quite ready to go to the Republican Conference and have a secret ballot vote about who should be Speaker. If the militants were determined to go to the floor and vote with the liberal Democrats, that was their prerogative. They could then go home and explain to their voters why they were turning power over to Dick Gephardt and David Bonior. I would listen to them and work with them, but I would not bargain over the speakership.

That Friday afternoon several of the leaders met with the militants. They had a very difficult and painful session. Up to that point the militants had been perhaps inadvertently encouraged in their discontent. Now they were being informed unequivocally that the entire leadership group would reject their plan and fight them in the Conference. Based on what I heard later, I believe that some of them felt that they had been lied to and betrayed, that they had been talked into venturing out on a limb and were suddenly having the limb sawed off behind them. I also believe that for their part, the leaders had not at all intended for it to work out this way. They may have been clumsy, and in any case, in a situation like this, feelings are bound to be injured and finger-pointing is inevitable.

I talked with some of my closest allies on the floor and was reassured that the vast base of the party was totally supportive of me. All the committee chairmen were called to a meeting by Bob Livingston and Jerry Solomon. They were unanimously for me. So I flew home knowing that we would win. Still, I was feeling almost the kind of sorrow you feel when there has been a death in the family. I had worked for nearly two decades to create a Republican House majority, and in three short years after it had finally happened, some of the people who had been part of that victory were so frustrated and upset that replacing me had seemed to them a reasonable thing to do.

I had survived a series of very hard campaigns, 120,000 negative commercials, a brutal ethics attack, and now I was in a fight within my own team. This was the experience that I was finding more painful than any in a whole career full of battles.

I flew home, and that evening Marianne and my daughter Kathy met me at a local restaurant that was always filled with supporters and friends. People kept coming by the table and saying things like "Don't give in" and "Keep it up." They thought that the source of my problem, as usual, was the Democrats and the press, but I could not get my mind off those sophomores who were so angry they would even consider splitting the party. What added most acutely to the pain was the fact that I truly admired many of those militants. After all, in my own career as a back-bencher I had been much like them. I had gone to the floor and taken the fight to the Democrats. I had argued publicly with my party leadership. And in 1990, even though I was Republican whip, I split with President Bush over the tax increase.

That Saturday I was still thinking about the militants and trying to figure out where things had gone so very wrong when I
began to get calls from other conservative activist members who
wanted to let me know that they were totally committed to
what we were doing and would do everything in their power to
talk their friends out of doing anything destructive. Two days
later, on Monday, the potential twenty or so rebels had shrunk to
ten, and even the holdouts were sending signals that they
wanted to work with us, that they had only been trying to send a
message about the intensity of their feelings. They asserted publicly that the idea of moving to vacate the Speaker's chair had
just been excited talk. They would never have done it.

That Wednesday we had a meeting of House Republicans to
elect two new members of leadership. Susan Molinari, vice chair
of the Republican Conference, was leaving the House, and Jennifer Dunn was leaving her position as conference secretary to
run for Susan's place. Jim Nussle was running against Jennifer;
and Deborah Pryce, Sue Myrick, Duke Cunningham, and Jerry
Weller were in a four-way race for Jennifer's job. The media had
reported these two races as tests of my strength: Jennifer was a
strong ally, and Jim Nussle had publicly complained about the
leadership. Nussle was a dear friend. I had picked him to manage
the transition in the House in 1994. I had helped to get him on
the Ways and Means Committee. I had campaigned for him in
his district. He came to me a few days before the election and
offered to withdraw from the race if I thought that would stop
the talk about a possible coup. I urged him not to take the press
gossip seriously and to stay in. This was the loyalty of the person
the press was using as a barometer of the opposition to me. Both
Jennifer and Deborah Pryce won decisively and added to the
leadership two strong voices for party unity.

That very morning *The Hill* carried what turned out to be a fascinating blow-by-blow account of the coup attempt. The story enraged many members, though parts of it seemed exaggerated to me. Dick Armey and I both reassured the Conference that morning that the article was inaccurate. It turned out, however, that we did not know everything, and our reassurances merely undermined our own credibility. Later that day we learned that there was a lot more confusion and misunderstanding between the leaders and the militants than we had understood. Things had gone a lot farther than anyone had told me, certain of the leaders having decided that they owed their survival to listening and learning without involving me. The militants had been under the impression that they had more support than they turned out to have. Members were angry and calling one another names.

Bill Paxon was the only member of the senior leadership who had been appointed to his job by me rather than elected. He came to feel that he had not handled the situation the way he should and offered to resign. Bill is a terrific talent. He and his wife, Susan Molinari, are personal friends of Marianne's and mine. Bill has a great future in politics, as became clear to everyone when he played a key role in our winning the majority in 1994 and keeping it in 1996. Nevertheless, at that point it seemed best for him to step down. I accepted his resignation.

After this there was one final aftermath of all the plotting and maneuvering. The members insisted on a members-only conference to hear from each one of the leaders just what his role and responsibility had been. I had already talked individually with everyone involved in this averted calamity and felt assured that we were now going to work together effectively and rebuild our team. However, other members who had only read the articles and heard the rumors were not satisfied. They wanted the plotting and griping to end once and for all. Late in the evening we met in the Capitol. Two hundred members were present.

I thought for some time about how to open the meeting, knowing that feelings were raw and tempers were short. As I prepared, it was Trent Lott who brought me the most helpful advice. He told how he had been talking to his daughter the previous Sunday, complaining about someone who had crossed him and how he planned to retaliate. "You shouldn't think that way," she had said, and she pointed him to a passage from Romans, chapter 12, which she had heard that morning in church. As he heard of the uproar among House Republicans, Trent brought the same passage to me, and that night I opened my comments with these words: "Do not repay anyone evil for evil. Be careful to do what is right in the eyes of everybody. If it is possible, as far as it depends on you, live at peace with everyone." The next day, the papers referred to the evening as a revival-style meeting.

My speech was only the beginning. Each of the senior leaders told of what had happened and where they believed they had erred, some of them with real emotion. Some members demanded an explanation from the militants, who gave their own perspective. As the evening progressed, the room still held a great deal of tension, and we ran the risk of degenerating into bitterness. At that point, Sonny Bono, the former TV and singing star and, for all too brief a time, congressman from California, asked to be recognized.

Sonny had a great gift for engaging people with his humor. Under his shy smile and laid-back demeanor there lurked a great talent for keeping an audience listening. He began by saying that he thought we were in an identity crisis, and really had to come to grips with the fact that this Congress was not the last one ever. Then he began to tell the story of the end of his career as an entertainer, and everyone sat up to listen. He went, he said, from writing and performing gold records and producing one of the most popular television shows of the early 1970s to being only a guest performer. Indeed, he held the record for the most guest spots on *Fantasy Island*. He hated doing these guest spots, but he was reluctant to give up his career as an entertainer. He wryly described his descent from huge dressing room, to small dressing room, to shared dressing room, to permission to use the men's room.

Finally, he was given a guest role on *Fantasy Island* where he had only one line. He was supposed to say, "It's a nice day, Tattoo," but he messed up the line and said, "It's a nice day, Pontoon." The actor who played Tattoo, the late Herve Villechaize, was very irritated by the mistake and started to give Sonny a good deal of grief. As the harangue continued, Sonny thought to himself, "I've got eight gold records, and I'm taking all this crap from a midget."

His self-deprecating humor broke any remaining tension, as Sonny explained that the experience was "God's way of telling me to forget the past and move on." It was an experience that he himself had learned from, as he moved on to become a restaurant owner, then mayor of Palm Springs, and finally member of Congress. He told us to do the same.

Sonny was killed in a dreadful skiing accident in early January 1998. He will be missed more deeply than he in his modesty would perhaps ever have believed. And no one who was at that conference meeting—least of all me—will ever forget how he calmed us and how much we owed him.

We in the leadership now had a lot of thinking and regrouping to do, and we were very lucky to be able to rely on the energy and enthusiasm of both Jennifer and Deborah. We were also very fortunate that this was the time when negotiations on the budget and saving Medicare and cutting taxes were all coming to fruition. It felt as if the sun was at last beginning to break through.

By the time of the August break, we had passed all this legislation and the President was about to sign it. Some conservatives thought we had given Clinton too much in exchange for his signature, but as the members began to go home they discovered that the people were actually happy with the Republican Congress and were willing to give us the benefit of the doubt. Later, during the fall, we continued to make progress as we cut the bureaucratic red tape that was wound around the Food and Drug Administration and so accelerated the much needed distribution of new drugs and new medical technologies. We also launched the universally applauded campaign to overhaul the Internal Revenue Service, along with a nationwide debate about sweeping tax reform. By New Year's members around the country were reporting that their constituents were very positive.

This story of the coup-that-wasn't might seem an odd one for me to be telling, for in this case it was our militant sophomores and our leaders more than I who learned a lesson the hard way. During all that time, even when things were most painful, I couldn't, deep down, be truly angry. For two reasons.

First, one of the old movies I love to watch is *True Grit*. It is the story of a brave and determined young girl who hires a crusty old character named Rooster Cogburn (played by John Wayne) to undertake a difficult mission on her behalf. Throughout the movie they are in contention, because she means to go along on the mission come what may, and the John Wayne character wants her to stay behind where he believes young girls belong. But he can't shake her. Wherever he goes, there she is. In one scene John Wayne and Glen Campbell are crossing a river on a ferry raft. They watch as the girl plunges her horse into the river, determined to stay on their heels. Wayne looks at her, turns to Campbell, and says, "She reminds me of me."

How could I, who had spent years trying to move the party faster than its senior leadership wanted it to move, stay truly mad at someone who was driven by the same passion? If I had been one of the militant sophomores, my heart might very well have been with them.

My second reason is one you would best understand if you talked to any former Democrat who now serves in the House Republican Conference. He will tell you about the change from a political machine that manages through coercion to a conference that decides through competition and open dialogue. In other words, what we had been suffering were actually some further growing pains in the coming-of-age of a new and very different kind of party. I call it the entrepreneurial party.

CHAPTER 10

BUILD AN
ENTREPRENEURIAL
PARTY

W<small>E HAD COME THROUGH A LOT</small>, my fellow Republican House members and I. It was not just a matter of one personality or another behaving in this way or that. Something bigger was involved. No one knew this better than the former Democrats who joined us. For we are actually a whole new kind of party finding our way into the future. Nobody understood this better than they. It's not just that Democrats and Republicans are two opposing parties fighting each other for power, as political parties normally do. Nor is it just that we disagree with each other on matters of policy. It is that we have entirely different conceptions of what we are and how we operate.

According to our ex-Democrats, the Democratic Caucus is entirely dominated by the party's left wing. Members who speak in terms of values considered the slightest bit conservative are at the very least made uncomfortable. The pressures either to conform or to keep quiet are practically insurmountable. In short, the caucus has become a kind of machine.

The Republican Conference, on the other hand—in the years I have been in Congress—has been just that, a gathering of equals expected to carry on an open discussion. In the minds of the senior Republicans the distinction to be drawn is that between a political pressure cooker and a partnership of people whose rights were to be protected.

After we became the majority, we discovered why conformity and compliance were so highly valued by our predecessors. The minority seldom has to win. It needs simply to do the best it can and to oppose the majority. The majority party, however, has the obligation to win virtually every vote every day. A minimum requirement just to keep the legislative process alive is to pass the rules that govern the bringing up of bills. Moreover, if the majority is to keep control of the House floor, beating back appeals of the rulings of the chair and winning on motions for the previous question are essential. Beyond that, if the majority wishes to pass its program, it is indispensable to win key amendments, to defeat substitutes offered by the minority, and to win again on final passage.

The minute we became a majority, we began to realize that the pressures on us to round up votes were enormously greater. Over time this pressure to get things done tends to push the majority into the mode of inducing conformity. Thus there is a permanent danger that like the animals in George Orwell's *Animal Farm*, we might gradually come to resemble the very machine we had replaced.

Still, even under all this pressure, there are basic differences between us and the Democrats that make it possible for us to remain a free debating society while being the majority. This has to do with the nature of our view of power, the kind of people we recruit, and our belief about what leads to the best long-term result. To begin with, the Democrats are a traditional political party while the Republicans tend to be a party of policy. Second, Democrats far more than Republicans are attracted to power and view politics as a profession with its own unique requirements and rewards. They first wish to acquire, and then to use, power. It is not that they have no ideology: They seek to maintain the liberalism that for so many years of the twentieth century held the United States government in thrall. But the truth is, they desire power more than they worry about policy. In other words, they treat one another as politicians.

By contrast, the Republican Party is essentially a party of policy. To some extent this has been true of the Republican Party since its founding in the 1850s as the party of freedom and union. Where big city machines in the North and county courthouse machines in the South were Democratic and tended to dominate the tone of the party's activists, there were many fewer machine politicians in the Republican Party. It was in large measure the party of people who cared about some policy or other and wanted to acquire power so they could bring it to bear on what they cared about in the real world. There were remarkably few Republicans who sought power for its own sake and were thus natural politicians. In other words, the Democratic Party is in its nature more a purely political creation, with all the strengths and weaknesses that implies, while the Republican Party has on the whole been less strictly power oriented and hence less flexible about its principles, with all the strengths and weaknesses that implies.

Thus the Democratic Party tends to recruit people who see politics as a career rather than a form of public service. Very often politics is seen by Democrats as a way to higher status and greater wealth. Many of them have spent their early years studying how to be successful politicians by serving in a kind of apprenticeship to those who are already successful at politics.

On the other hand, at least nowadays, Republican politicians tend to be people who have been successful at other things first, and who have gone into the business of running for office to achieve certain ends. They spend more of their time thinking and talking about policy and less of it discussing the mechanics and arts of gaining political power. If they succeed at what they are after, they are happy. Many of them pride themselves on not being desperate for office and unwilling to modify their views merely for the sake of succeeding. "I don't need to be here" is a sentiment heard far more often in the Republican Conference than in the Democratic Caucus.

One other thing differentiates them. Since the Democrats are liberals in a system that had been shaped by liberalism for something like half a century, they are under no pressure to change, only to expand. On most days what they need are not new ideas but simply more votes for the old ones. Republicans on the other hand are looking to innovate. They want to break down the old system and return the power it has usurped to the people for whom it was intended. Therefore we cannot simply stay in power but must find better ways, for example, for the country to make itself focus on the creation of new wealth instead of remaining preoccupied with the means of redistributing what wealth already exists. We believe we must help American society prepare itself for the radical changes in the areas of life that are being wrought now and far into the future by microchips and fiber optics. Just winning votes, then, is not what we are about. Nor is merely acting to stop the liberals. We need to be proactive, that is, we need new ideas and lots of them. We need a continuing debate in which these ideas can be modified, improved, and tested.

This requires a very different mode of operation for the House Republican Conference. If we allow the pressures of being a majority to push us into the kind of machine politics that is so largely characteristic of the Democratic Caucus, we will be sealing our own doom. We need to encourage, not discourage, independent thinking. We must welcome dissent and argument rather than attempt to suppress them. In other words, we do not need spear carriers of conformity but entrepreneurs of social policy.

This recognition of what the Republican Party is and needs to be is what kept me from being vindictive over the plots of summertime. The leadership of a party whose mandate is to be entrepreneurial must hold people together by listening carefully and by persuasion. For me to fall into the habits of a machine boss would be an even greater defeat than losing the speakership. It would be precisely a betrayal of the ideals for whose sake we worked so hard to come into power.

I had no desire to punish the militants for their idealism and impatience. But I did want to help them learn how to make their expenditure of energy effective—something, I say with great pleasure, that began to happen as they dominated the floor in the week we spent offering amendments to a major appropriations bill. Nor did I want to push anyone out of the leadership. We have been the most successful Republican leadership team in sixty-eight years. But I knew that I had the responsibility to rebuild the group into a coherent, trusting, and productive team once again.

By October 1997, we had proved ourselves to be back on track.

My commitment to help the Republicans become the kind of entrepreneurial party I have described grew from what might seem an unlikely source. In the fall of 1982, Marianne and I were in New York to meet with Richard Nixon. We spent about three hours with him. I told him I thought the Republicans at long last ought to become the majority in the House. He shook his head and said that the House Republican Party had little impact and received little attention from the press because it was so boring. It was already boring when he served in the House, from 1946 to 1950. "If you really want to become the majority," he said, "you have to fill the place with ideas. No one person can do that," he added; "so go back and organize a group that will meet at least once a month, and, say, have dinner in Georgetown or some-place like that and talk about ideas."

We discussed this suggestion all the way home, and decided to act on it. As soon as we got back to Washington, I recruited a group of idea-oriented, activist congressmen. We called our-selves the Conservative Opportunity Society. We met once a week on Wednesday mornings. Our chief sponsor was Trent Lott, then the House Republican Whip. Guy Vander Jagt pro-vided supporting resources through the Congressional Cam-paign Committee. Our goal was to create a Republican Party capable of remaining responsive to the changing needs of a changing world. We recognized that in the world in which we live you can't just have a simple ideology and plan. When you solve a particular problem, your solution itself leaves you with new problems. Social philosophers call this "the unintended con-sequences of social action." We must have goals, of course, but the process (along with your mind) needs to be open and flex-ible. That way people can attack problems from a variety of angles and make their respective contributions without being stymied by the obstacle of some time-honored practice. Many a great business enterprise, as we know, has atrophied from losing its founding entrepreneurial spirit and becoming merely managerial. That has been even more the case in Washington.

I see my work as Speaker as a form of venture capitalism. I try to spend my time, the authority of my office, and my personal resources on nurturing people who over time can become important developers of ideas. Take the case of Mark Neumann, a Wisconsinite who arrived in the House with the class of 1994. He had never served in public office before and was one of the most rigid members of his class. He was as determined as he was passionate. For many months he made a great deal of trouble. He is also extraordinarily bright, and has a determination to balance the budget second only to John Kasich's. When his intensity and rigidity threatened to get him into more trouble than he could handle, I worked with him and asked others to mentor him. I admired his passionate determination to save his children from deficit spending and his raw courage in taking on the legislative system when he thought it was wrong. Because he was allowed to work through his ideas while learning the ropes, he has emerged as a major leader in dealing with the budget. We need many more Mark Neumanns.

It is instructive to compare what we are trying to do with the Republican Party of yore. There were perhaps two or three people who were pledged for life to their ideas, such as Henry Hyde with his commitment to the right to life and Jack Kemp with his belief in economic growth. Such people were few, and they tended to be so different from the norm that they can't be replicated. They keep going by virtue of their special talents and their own iron will.

However, we need not a few stars but an army of people willing to make a difference. As a small example, if we could have a different individual who met our standard of Republicanism appear each week on each of the Sunday morning talk shows, we might effect a notable shift in the climate of opinion. This requires both a Republican Conference and a speakership open to a lot of diversity and dissent. To the news media, of course, diversity and dissent look like trouble. Since they positively thrive on our difficulties, any hint of disagreement among us becomes a big story. This is a nuisance for us but if we are going to be serious about pursuing our goals, we will just have to learn to live with it.

In truth, when it comes to the kind of ferment I believe a party like ours needs, we are even now 10 to 20 percent below where we should be. We are living on the brink of a huge transition, from the industrial age to the information age. We do not yet understand what will be needed for people to have a free, decent, and comfortable life in this new age. In the information age, we won't need twenty or thirty people to lead us but four or five hundred.

All of which leads me to be very tolerant of long meetings. I must confess that it also leads me to favor newer members who have ideas over more senior members who don't. One of the jobs of the Speaker is to select the person assigned to answer the President's State of the Union address. The year I first became Speaker, the response was given by Christine Todd Whitman, the newly elected governor of New Jersey. In 1997 it was the then-sophomore J. C. Watts, a brilliant young comer in the party. One of my more pressing entrepreneurial goals is to keep putting more and more new talent out on the hustings for the world to see. All of this seems to confuse a lot of people, particularly when they hear me saying nice things about our more dissident members. I would be less than honest if I denied that these dissidents sometimes infuriate me and have on occasion made my life, to put it mildly, difficult. But they do so because they have guts, and along with guts comes the ambition to spread one's wings, and that is something I consider essential not only for the Republican Party but for the United States of America.

One of the things that helped us at long last to put the Democratic Party in the minority, aside, that is, from the fact that they were simply no longer paying the slightest attention to the anxieties and needs of the American people, is the way they isolate and punish dissenters from their strict party line. This is a time-honored practice on the left, where dissent of any kind is always viewed as either a threat or a sin. Thus they deprive themselves of many possible sources of new energy. Since our ranks are now swelled with ex-Democrats who could no longer bear to march in lockstep, we are the happy beneficiaries of their demand for conformity. Almost four hundred elected Democrats, including two United States senators and five House members, have joined our ranks since Clinton won the presidency in 1992.

In some ways the most obvious example of what I mean by entrepreneurial leadership in the House is John Kasich. His father had worked in the post office before he was killed in an automobile accident, along with John's mother, about ten years ago. John had always been a precocious kid. While he was still in college, he was elected to the Ohio legislature. He was also the only Republican to defeat a Democratic incumbent in 1982.

As these facts by themselves would suggest, he is also very energetic and aggressive. The main focus of his militancy is the budget. He is perhaps more intent than anyone in the Congress on balancing the budget, shrinking the size of government, and reducing the national debt. He first came to public attention when he introduced a bill to kill the B–2 bomber. For Kasich, it was strictly a matter of wasting money on a program that he thought made no sense once the Cold War was over. In his mind the B–2 was originally designed as a deterrent to a Soviet nuclear strike. With the dissolution of the Soviet Union it simply made no sense to build such an expensive system. An anti–defense spending conservative is something of an anomaly, and Kasich received a great deal of attention in the media for his leadership on this issue. I actually disagreed with John about the usefulness of a very long-range manner bomber that could penetrate sophisticated defenses with minimum risk. We debated the issue several times on the House floor. While we disagreed, I admired his thoughtfulness and his courage in taking on this issue and working at it so consistently.

When I was whip, Kasich was a member of the Budget Committee. He actually drew up his own budget and got thirty-three votes for it. I worked against it, on the ground that it was too radical, but again I had to admire his energy and his initiative. In 1993, when Bill Gradison resigned from the Budget Committee, Kasich became the committee's ranking Republican. He wanted to offer a detailed and very different budget from the tax-increase-higher-spending budget the Democrats were proposing. A number of Republicans wanted simply to spend their time attacking the Democratic tax increase. But John felt that he had to have a detailed alternative budget if the news media were going to take us seriously. I agreed with Kasich. In fact, his strategy paralleled one we had followed in 1979 and 1980, when I had worked with David Stockman and Jack Kemp on what we called the Budget of Hope and Opportunity, which foreshadowed the Reagan program of 1981. Kasich was doing the right thing, even though it took an enormous amount of effort and the willingness to work through many disagreements with colleagues. He and I agreed that we could not simply be an opposition minority party. We had to be an alternative governing party. In a very real sense, this struggle over the budget led to the approach that eventuated in the Contract With America.

Someone who has never been a member of the House of Representatives might find it difficult to assess just how extraordinary John's career has been. He went from being a back-bencher to being a ranking committee member, which is a big stretch. From there, in 1995 he became Budget Chairman, which is an even bigger one. He was then negotiating with Senate Budget Committee chairman Pete Domenici, very much senior to him, and then along with Pete Domenici negotiating with the White House. All in four years. My friend John Uhlmann had told me to be careful about how I used the word "grow" in Washington, but if growing is not the right word for John Kasich, I don't know what is.

In 1994 we offered another Republican budget alternative. At the same time we developed the Contract With America, we began to talk about having a balanced budget by the year 2002. Our principle was that we supported a constitutional amendment requiring a balanced budget, with an effective date of 2002. But if we really meant that the budget should be in balance by 2002, then whether the amendment passed or not, we ourselves should do it. The country liked this promise of ours, along with the others, and we became a majority.

When we did, John Kasich became chairman of the Budget Committee. Now we had to write a budget that would actually shrink government, cut taxes, and be in balance by 2002. As you may guess, translating political principle into legislative reality was no stroll in the park. It involved a lot of pain and a lot of conflict. One day John came to a leadership meeting and said it would be almost impossible to balance the budget in seven years. "I don't think you guys looked at how hard it's going to be," he said to us. Whereupon we all said to him, "We understand that, John, that's why you're chairman. We trust your energy and intelligence. You'll be able to get it done." "No," he said, "you guys don't understand. You haven't looked at the details. Anyway, who said 2002 was written in stone?" I said, "That's a great question. Who thinks it's written in stone?" When we all raised our hands, John looked at us with incredulity. That spring we had a retreat in Leesburg, Virginia, and we gave Kasich a marble plaque with "Budget 2002" chiseled on it.

I have told the story of John Kasich's rise and impact because he is emblematic of what I mean by an entrepreneurial party. You can see that it is difficult and sometimes pretty messy. The difference between such a party and an ordinary one is like the difference between a bureaucracy and the floor of the stock market. True, there is a fair amount of friction and uncertainty, but there is by the same token a lot of creativity and the capacity to respond quickly to entirely new situations.

An example of what I mean by flexibility is our response to the tobacco negotiation and its implementing legislation. When the trial lawyers, attorneys general for the states, and the tobacco industry reached their private agreement, they were breaking a lot of new ground. There were public policy implications involving many major congressional committees. This was a multiyear, multibillion-dollar undertaking, which is only beginning as I write. We decided that we needed a very special task force to coordinate the development of the overall legislation as well as to assess whether it was the right thing to do, and if so, what was the right way to do it.

I asked Congresswoman Deborah Pryce, a former judge who is a member of the Rules Committee and an elected member of the leadership, to chair the task force. The task force members include Scott McInnis from the Rules Committee; Bill Archer, chairman of the Ways and Means Committee; Henry Hyde, chairman of the Judiciary Committee; Tom Bliley, chairman of the Commerce Committee; Bob Smith of the Agriculture Committee; and John Kasich of the Budget Committee. And there it is, a brand-new working group that ties together six committees and the elected leadership to represent the members so they can all work together. We have done the same thing with the war on drugs, and something similar to design the Medicare reform bill in 1995.

Another example of entrepreneurship was Vern Ehlers's remarkable achievement between Election Day 1994 and the day after our swearing-in in January 1995. In less than two months' time Vern had worked with James Billington, the Librarian of Congress, to develop an Internet system for the United States House of Representatives. It is called Thomas after Thomas Jefferson, and it allows anyone in the world to access information and House records through the Internet. In its first month it had 2 million users. Vern is a physicist, the only one in Congress, and he had helped to computerize the Michigan legislature when he served there. He is a man with a unique ability to get a job done right, and get it done quickly.

Thanks to Vern's efforts, one of the proudest moments in my career came in the summer of 1997, when Bill Archer got up on the floor of the House and announced, "I am now filing the tax bill. Within thirty seconds it will be available to every American through the Internet without having to call a lobbyist or a trade association or pay for a subscription to any service." This is the true grassroots populism of the information age. It was a wonderful moment, and within a few hours over 200,000 citizens had downloaded the tax bill onto their computers. Lobbyists had the experience of getting phone calls from back home in which the clients to whom they were speaking had the bill in front of them and knew as much or more about the details as their Washington "specialists." This was the dawning of a new day in representative self-government.

This spirit of flexibility and speed is in a deeply American tradition. In World War II it took us only ninety-three days to design and field the P–51 Mustang. Remind those who run the Pentagon today, who could not, or perhaps would not, do something like that in less than seven to twelve years. The United States government was able to get it done in 1944 because the environment was one in which those in charge of the country could simply say, "Figure out how, and do it." Somehow those who were given the task figured out how. It should not be necessary for us to be at war to be able to recapture that spirit and style of operation.

As I look around the House Republican Conference today, I see more and more examples of entrepreneurial behavior. There is Dana Rohrabacher, helping to revolutionize transportation into space with his persistent support for the single-stage-to-orbit vehicle. George Nethercutt is dramatically improving health for diabetics. Duncan Hunter is our leader in building triple fences along the American border so illegal drugs and illegal immigrants can be kept from entering the country. John Porter has dramatically increased resources for biomedical research. Rick Lazio is improving the quality of life for citizens in public housing and is pioneering a dramatic transformation in housing for the poor. Tillie Fowler is playing a leading role in bringing common sense to the military with respect to the roles of the two sexes. JoAnn Emerson is bringing a solution-oriented approach to environmental issues as they affect rural America. Rob Portman has been a dual entrepreneur in working to create drug-free communities and in chairing the commission to reform the IRS.

There is a new spirit of grassroots inventiveness and activism that is bringing waves of new ideas into the House Republican Conference. I cannot foresee exactly where all this will lead, but I am certain we will have ever better proposals to make to the American people and ever better solutions for their problems in the course of the next few years. Perhaps the news media will even become more interested in what we are actually doing and less in the inevitably messy process involved in our figuring out how to do it.

We need social policy entrepreneurs because we should be preparing to move to a more productive, more prosperous, safer, and freer America. A tall order, I know, and one that has at least one major hurdle to overcome.

CHAPTER 11

STAY ON OFFENSE

BILL BENNETT HAS SAID IT BEST: Either you are on offense or you are on defense. There are no time-outs, no huddles, no half-times; every minute of every day of every week, you are either moving forward or being forced to protect yourself.

The longer one is engaged in government and politics, the truer Bill's words come to seem. When you are defining the issue and setting the terms of the debate—when you are on offense—your allies are confident and your opponents are picking up the pieces. But if we let our opponents (who are likely to number among them the news media) choose the ground of battle, our allies will become anxious and restless and wonder if we know what we are doing.

Take the case of the Bush presidential campaign in 1988. Bush was going to have no easy row to hoe. For one thing, no

sitting Vice President had been elected President since Martin
Van Buren succeeded Andrew Jackson in 1836. For another
thing, in May 1988 he was nineteen points behind Governor
Michael Dukakis—the man who would win the Democratic
nomination to run against him—touted by the media as the brilliant technocrat who had been responsible for the "Massachusetts miracle" of economic development and was pioneering a
new, smarter liberalism that was going to rejuvenate the Democratic Party. In other words, the odds against Bush's becoming
President seemed pretty long as we entered the summer of 1988.

What happened then was a sight to see: a campaign based on
a deep understanding of what was going on in the country combined with an unshakable will to remain tactically on the offensive. The author of this campaign was Lee Atwater, the most
creative and most intense professional in the Republican Party.
Lee was a unique combination of abilities. He had a South Car-
olinian's taste for barbecue, an adventurer's love for motorcycles,
an intellectual's deep understanding of Machiavelli, and a lifetime devotion to politics shaped by Senator Strom Thurmond
and Governor Carroll Campbell. Lee was both a great strategist
and a marvelous tactician. He succeeded in getting, and keeping,
the Democrats on the defensive.

There was a brief flurry right after the Republican conven-
tion, when the press jumped on Dan Quayle and tried to score
negative points out of his nomination, but within a few days the
Republican team was able to regain the initiative and then hang
on to it.

If Dukakis had had the feel for what moved the American
people that had once been displayed by a fellow citizen of Massachusetts named John F. Kennedy, and if he had been able to
stick to it, he might have won. For Kennedy had run as a hawk

(by, among other things, inventing a nonexistent "missile gap") and a hot advocate of economic growth ("Get the country moving again") and had found the way to the hearts of many people who would a generation later become the Reagan Democrats. Dukakis, however, was not Kennedy, and from almost the first moment, he had allowed himself to be put on the defensive.

So what was this campaign that carried Bush from nineteen points behind in May to eight points ahead by Election Day? With the dreadfully premature loss of Atwater to cancer, nothing like it would be provided for President Bush in 1992. In any case, it seems to me especially useful for people interested in politics, particularly conservative politics, to recall the summer of 1988. We knew, first of all, that the Democratic ticket would lose if the voters could be convinced that Dukakis was simply an old-style Massachusetts liberal. We knew also that the traditional strategy of moderate Republicans—to campaign by moving ever closer to the center—would never work: The conservative activists needed for Bush to win would just stay home. It was essential, then, to define Bush on the right and to get Dukakis defined as well left of center. On the Bush side, the quickest way to do this was with the issue of taxes. Bush said, "Read my lips: no new taxes!" and the conservatives were reassured.[1]

Defining Dukakis as left of center turned out to be not all that difficult a task. The first thing that was done was to make a point of his membership in the American Civil Liberties Union

---

[1]That was why it was so devastating to his chances for reelection in 1992 when he broke that pledge in 1990 and allowed himself to be persuaded that raising taxes would not be a big deal. Interestingly, virtually every conservative government around the world that raised taxes suffered the same consequences. Margaret Thatcher cites this as a "rule" of conservative politics.

(ACLU). Now, as it happens, the ACLU is an organization with a long and distinguished history of fighting to protect freedom of speech. On the other hand, in recent years it has carried its mandate to ever more eccentric and often highly destructive lengths. While it may have been perfectly honorable for Dukakis to belong to the ACLU, it was equally legitimate for Bush to attack him for it. And with what enormous relish he did the job!

Another thing with which Dukakis could be marked as a liberal was a program to register prisoners to vote. By 1988 ever growing numbers of Americans were losing faith in the possibility of rehabilitating criminals and were taking a tough line on crime and on the need for incarcerating the guilty to protect the innocent. Worrying about whether people in prison had the right to vote was the wrong worry as far as they were concerned.

But prisoner voting rights was a pale pastel issue compared with another program that could be laid at Dukakis's door, namely, granting weekend furloughs to prisoners who had been convicted of crimes of violence up to and including murder. This idea was so lacking in common sense that even in isolation it could have done a lot of damage to Dukakis. But taken in the context of a general liberal extremism, it was devastating. Our focus groups told us that the Reagan Democrats—who still did not feel at home in the Republican Party and without whom, of course, Bush would be beaten—were willing to forgive Dukakis one liberal failing. A couple more made them very uneasy; but by the time they got to, say, four, they were decisively with Bush. One woman summed up the situation perfectly when she said of one of Dukakis's programs, "Why, if that were true, he'd be a liberal, and I could never vote for a liberal."

The murderers' furlough program became the most famous

because it was the most vivid, the most shocking, and probably, above all, because ultimately the media focused on it to discredit the Republican victory. You may remember Willy Horton, a murderer who while on furlough kidnapped, tortured, and raped a woman (and tortured her fiancé) in Maryland. The problem, however, was that Willy Horton was black, thus giving the press and the Dukakis campaign an opening to accuse the Bush campaign of racism. Which they proceeded to do with hammer and tongs. So relentless were they, indeed, that they drove Roger Ailes, Bush's brilliant communications director, out of the politics business altogether (and, ironically, into a much bigger career in television).

If this offensive was depressing to Ailes, it was positively infuriating to me because it was simply a big lie. I know how the issue of murderers' furloughs had evolved because I myself had played a role in it. The issue had nothing whatever to do with Willy Horton's being black and was exclusively concerned with his being a vicious killer who enjoyed torturing and raping. As it happened, in late May or early June 1988, I was told about the furlough program by an acquaintance who had just read an article written by a friend for *Reader's Digest,* entitled "Getting Away With Murder." The article, said my acquaintance, proved just how wildly liberal the Dukakis Administration in Massachusetts had been. Willy Horton's name did not even come up in that conversation. Then I learned that the Lawrence, Massachusetts, *Eagle-Tribune* had won a Pulitzer for an investigative series about the release of murderers on weekend furloughs. Moreover, it turned out that even after the program had become controversial, Dukakis had vetoed a bill to repeal it. This was clearly his program.

Next I read the entire newspaper series into the *Congressional*

Record, which required several hours of special orders over a
two-week period. I kept inviting the Democratic members from
Massachusetts to come to the floor to defend their governor's
program, but no one took up my invitation. In this series, Willy
Horton just happened to be one of several murderers who committed crimes while out on furlough. And when *Reader's Digest*
came out in early July, it had an immediate and powerful effect.
Within a week of the magazine's arrival in the mail, Dukakis
began to drop in the polls. (What a tribute to the power of that
magazine!)

Willy Horton came to symbolize the issue because he was
given a prominent role in the *Digest* article. He had been in
prison for killing a young man by stabbing him twenty-two
times and dumping his body into a fifty-gallon oil drum. When
he received his furlough, he left Massachusetts and traveled to
Maryland, where he kidnapped the couple who suffered his various assaults. The point about Willy Horton was that in fur-
loughing him, Dukakis's program had put not just the citizens of
Massachusetts but everybody in the country at risk. So Willy
Horton was the most vivid symbol of the furlough program.
Outside the Bush campaign there were people who were exam-
ining the story with outrage. As for the Bush campaign itself, the
ads it ran about Willy Horton deliberately did not use his picture
but instead filmed people in prison costume walking through a
revolving door. Nevertheless the charge of racism stuck. The
elite media simply refused to accept the idea that a convicted
murderer who took advantage of being furloughed to rape and
torture a couple of people was a legitimate issue to confront.
There were certain columnists, for instance, who went so far as
to claim that it was unfair to Willy Horton to make him a symbol. In general, the fact that Dukakis had furloughed murderers

for the weekend was held to be out of bounds. To rule an issue out of order because it makes liberals uncomfortable—particularly when that issue happens to touch on people of color—is one of the forms of moral blackmail depended on to keep the understandings and feelings of most ordinary people from becoming a factor in elections.

Fortunately for then-Vice President Bush, his campaign and his supporters were not going to back off the issue of murderers' furloughs. Nor were they going to apologize for it. If the Bush campaign had flinched, it would have gone on permanent defense. By refusing to concede that the Willy Horton debate was about anything but the issue of releasing violent criminals and by insisting on remaining focused on it as an aspect of Dukakis's policy, the Bush campaign continued to move forward.

Whether the murderers' furlough plan by itself would have been enough to sink Dukakis we shall never know, though I myself am inclined to think it would not have been. But in combination with various other symptoms of Dukakis's liberalism, such as his refusal to ask the teachers of Massachusetts to recite the Pledge of Allegiance, it all came together to guarantee his defeat. The liberals clearly did not recognize the degree to which they were on the wrong side of a new wave of national emotion. Ridicule also helped: the image of Dukakis riding around in a tank to show his sudden passion for military strength; the image of the filth floating in Boston Harbor for the would-be leader of the party claiming devotion to cleaning up the environment. Both made people laugh at him, which is fatal for a candidate. But of very great importance is the fact that the Bush campaign remained on the offense and the Dukakis campaign had to spend its energy and substance on defense.

I had had my own first lesson in the need for staying on offense in August 1981. The Reagan Administration had had a very successful first seven months. They had passed some major legislation, including tax cuts and cuts in government spending. They had begun to rebuild the American military. At the end of July everything seemed to be working really well. Then the administration literally went on vacation for the month of August. They were mostly Californians, and they simply went back to California for a month.

In August 1981 the left launched a counterattack against Reagan's policies. The issue of the homeless, for example, was fashioned, polished, and honed to stand as a kind of perfect summation of Reagan's indifference to the poor.[2]

The point is that the difference in mood between July 1981 and October 1981 was staggering. In July Reaganism seemed the wave of the future, and our efforts to reduce the size of government and lower taxes for the sake of a healthy private-sector economy that would create more wealth and more jobs were seen to be good. By October Reaganism was being defined as cutting off vital services to the poor and transferring wealth from them to the rich. To some extent moderate Republicans who had always been uncomfortable with Reagan's Western-style conservatism now found themselves on the side of the news media. It took us a long time to recover the offensive after that August break.

What I learned then is that great movements can never go

---

[2]The terrible irony here is that homelessness in the country's major cities was to some considerable extent the result of a once much-touted liberal initiative, namely, the emptying of the institutions for the insane and the "reintegration" of their former patients into the "community."

on vacation or stop pushing. In other words, if you're not on offense, you're on defense.

The war-fighting doctrine of the German army was that only one-third of your forces should be used to defend against a surprise attack and the other two-thirds should immediately begin to plan a counterattack. General MacArthur's daring decision during the Korean War to land at Inchon, which would put American forces far behind the North Korean lines, was conceived when his staff was not certain that he could even stay in Korea by holding the Pusan perimeter. Caution would have dictated rushing all the forces to Pusan to defend it against North Korean attack. MacArthur understood that if he had the discipline to risk holding reinforcements back and using them to launch an entirely new and totally unexpected attack halfway up the Korean peninsula, he would have the opportunity to administer a stunning defeat to the entire North Korean army. Which, of course, in the event he did.

The same passion for staying on the offense marked the four greatest Civil War commanders, Grant, Jackson, Lee, and Sherman. All of them understood that wars are won by taking risks and that the side with the initiative always has a huge advantage.

Another example makes an especially vivid illustration of my point: the 1997 Teamsters' strike against the United Parcel Service (UPS). It illustrates in the same way the advantage to the side in a conflict that has the initiative and gets to define the terms.

I watched the Teamsters' strike against UPS with special interest. UPS corporate headquarters happens to be in my district. Years ago I spent a day in UPS uniform. I rode in a truck that picked up packages in Atlanta and flew in the airplane that carried them to Louisville, Kentucky. In Louisville I watched packages from all over the country being sorted, and then I flew back to Atlanta with packages headed there. UPS, as anyone whose job is to ship things knows, is a remarkably efficient company. Its drivers are well paid, and they do an amazing job, which requires them simultaneously to be customer service reps, salesmen, pickup and delivery people, and record keepers. The drivers are in fact the heart of the system. One of the noteworthy things about UPS is that it places great emphasis on promoting from within, and the management prides itself on the quality and effectiveness of its workforce. While UPS has been organized by the Teamsters and competes with nonunion companies (notably Federal Express), the senior management officials have always been confident that they could work with their unionized employees and remain highly profitable.

All this was put to the test in 1997, when management officials found themselves in a negotiation followed by a strike that they literally did not understand. They approached the strike as a question of corporate economics and salaries and benefits for their workforce. They thought they had a strong economic case and were offering a positive package of economic incentives. I suspect they really did not expect a strike or at least did not expect that it would be very long. They had always had a good relationship with the Teamsters and expected negotiations to be hard but fruitful. Consequently, they had no worst-case plan for the fight they found themselves in. Furthermore, as leaders of a company that depended on a cohesive workforce to maintain the speed and efficiency that were their hallmarks, they were reluctant to get into an all-out fight. They wanted a clean settlement so they could concentrate on their new competitor, the United States Post Office.

But while UPS senior management saw the negotiations as a

solvable problem, their opponent at the bargaining table, namely Ron Carey, at that time president of the Teamsters, saw himself in a totally different situation. His extremely narrow reelection to the union presidency was about to be overturned for illegal campaign practices, and he may already have known it. In any case, his victory had been so narrow (he actually lost in the United States and won with Canadian votes) that he needed an emotional victory over UPS to give himself a boost in the eyes of his union members. And there was another bit of union business extraneous to the affairs of UPS that played a part. Carey was also the linchpin to John Sweeney's control of the AFL-CIO, which Sweeney in turn had also won by a narrow margin. Carey's competitor for the presidency, Jimmy Hoffa, Jr., was apt to take the Teamsters in a more independent direction. Moreover, Carey had been totally supportive of the Clinton ticket in both 1992 and 1996. So the ripples from the UPS negotiation went far beyond the bargaining table—indeed, all the way up to the White House. Everybody on the left had his own reasons for needing the Teamsters to win.

Carey had prepared a very well-conceived public relations campaign designed to put the UPS management in the worst possible light and to keep them there. By the time the UPS management began to realize just how badly they were losing the public relations fight, the battle was almost over. They would have had to take a long strike that might well have permanently crippled the company (which after all depends on the ability to service small and medium-sized business every twenty-four hours).

An equally well-planned and equally aggressive campaign on the part of UPS might have brought a different outcome. But the fact is that Carey had much more at stake than the UPS executives. He was fighting for his very survival while they were fighting to keep their company ever more prosperous and successful.

As soon as the strike ended, the federal elections supervisor declared that there had been so much corruption in Carey's election campaign that the election would have to be thrown out and a new one held, and ultimately it was found that Carey himself was so tainted that he could no longer be a candidate at all. So in the end, being on offense wasn't of much help to him. For UPS management, however, it ought still to have been an important lesson.

Another, and in some ways the most curious, example of the difference in consequence between offense and defense is to be found in the saga of the Clinton health plan. The Clintons, you may remember, launched this plan with high hopes and much fanfare. At first they did well, but then the terms of the debate were turned on them. Which is to say, when the issue under discussion was coverage for people who had no health insurance, their advocacy went very well, for the government seemed a reasonable answer to the problem. When, however, the issue became one of Americans turning over their own health care to the government, that was a very different matter. What had seemed a bold gamble in 1993 was by the summer of 1994 a complete bust. Be it noted, however, that the liberals who favored the Clinton plan did not give up just because the original plan crashed and burned. Government-run health care had first been proposed by President Harry Truman in 1949. Clearly it is an idea whose time has come and gone several times over the past half-century.

The secret is that liberals never take no for an answer. They lick their wounds, try to figure out what went wrong, and start over. By 1996 they were back with the Kennedy-Kassebaum health plan, a plan that would have significantly expanded government involvement. We were able to dilute Kennedy-Kassebaum and to establish medical savings accounts; nevertheless, they had taken some steps toward more government-run health care. Then in 1997 the President came back with the idea of providing health care for the poorest children not covered by any form of health insurance. We were able to stop the Washington-based bureaucracy proposed and to ensure that any new program would be run at the state level rather than the federal level. At the state level there would be a range of flexible choices rather than one general mandate. The point is, however, that the liberals one way and another managed to stay focused on expanding government involvement in health care.

Every conservative should take a lesson from the liberals in the uses of deliberate, sustained, permanent offense. Ever since they became a majority in 1930, the liberals have learned to keep taking as much as they can get in the way of legislation every day. A model for this is Ted Kennedy. Truth to tell, I have grown to respect the way he handles the process. You may not like him or his politics, but it is hard not to take your hat off to the steady, tough-minded, straightforward way he pushes for what he wants. As soon as we Republicans became the majority in the Senate, Kennedy realized he needed allies on the Republican side and began reaching out to them. He never quits looking for new opportunities to expand the government, and he is remarkably skilled at getting Republicans to sign on to bills with him. We on our side are as yet not nearly as tenacious, as firm, as clear about our ends, nor as clever in our tactics as the good senator; and any would-be conservative legislative leader could learn a lot about permanently being on offense by studying his ability to get hit, attacked, dismissed, and smilingly keep moving forward.

This need to be continuously moving forward was brought home to me in the fall of 1997 when I heard New Jersey governor Christie Whitman analyze the razor-thin margin of her reelection. She said her biggest problem was that she had failed to give the voters of New Jersey any clear sense of where she wanted to take them and their state in her second term. Instead of offering a bold vision of a better future for the state, she ran a relatively passive campaign in which she emphasized how much she had already gotten done and what a good person she was. Americans tend almost always to be future-oriented. They are more interested in what you are going to do for them next than in what you did for them last.

When you can be clear about where you are going, all of your allies can be clear about how they can help. In 1988 we were clear that we wanted to focus on how liberal Dukakis was and how far he would move the country away from the policies of Reagan-Bush. This made it possible for a lot of people to get involved and communicate this message in their own way.

In 1994 the Contract With America provided the clarity behind which people were able both to campaign and to help organize the first hundred days of the congressional session. That is exactly the kind of clarity I hope we will have as we face the new century full of hopes and plans for America's future.

CHAPTER 12

GOALS FOR A GENERATION

DESPITE THE FACT THAT THERE have been a few bumps along the way, we have reason to look back on the years since we took control of the House in 1994 with considerable satisfaction. The United States government, for instance, is now clearly moving to a balanced budget for the first time in nearly thirty years. Interest rates have fallen, which in turn has helped the economy grow (lower interest rates being almost as good as a tax cut). This growing economy, with 8 million new jobs, has produced the lowest rate of unemployment in twenty-seven years; the highest family income in history; and the highest farm income in history. The stock market has doubled in value, and the country is enjoying the lowest rate of violent crime in twenty-four years.

Finally, tax cuts have been enacted for the first time in sixteen years—smaller ones than we and our fellow Americans would have liked, but not negligible, including a $500 per child tax credit, cuts in the capital gains and death taxes, and new tax breaks for college and vocational-technical students. We have also saved Medicare without raising taxes for at least a decade, which should give us time to figure out how to correct this important program for the baby boomers and their children.

The scale of change we have enacted is illustrated by the story of fiscal 1997 (October 1, 1996, to September 30, 1997). In January 1996 the Congressional Budget Office projected a deficit for 1997 of $140 billion. In the end, the actual deficit was $23 billion. That is an improvement of $117 billion within a twenty-one-month period. We can, of course, never be absolutely certain that no unforeseen contingency will arise. Still, the improvement in the experts' calculation in 1997 should be enough to allay most doubts about the path of the deficit.

If America remains at peace, we can have a generation of government surpluses. That will happen if the liberals are not permitted to sponge up the surplus dollars on devising programs to keep the government growing beyond its means.

There is now a basic understanding that a free market combined with limited government works beneficially for society, economically, socially, and politically, from top to bottom. Not all governments act on this knowledge, of course, because what many of them are after is the permanent consolidation of their own power rather than the welfare of their citizens. But intellectually, the argument over centralized and command-and-control bureaucracies is over. Free markets and individual liberty won.

This historic new situation is by itself, of course, a great opportunity. But there is much left to be done to prepare ourselves properly for it. Consider, for example, what recently happened to Marianne. She went out to buy something that cost her $15 and had to wait an hour and a half in line to do it. She was actually lucky, she said, because she had called around and determined that this was the shortest line available for her purchase. At two other suppliers there would have been a wait of up to two and a half hours. What Marianne was doing was renewing her Georgia driver's license. With the possible exception of the hottest fads of the moment (such as Beanie Babies, or the newest "in" restaurant, or a ticket to a rock concert), where in the private sector could anyone selling something get their customers to wait in line for an hour and a half?

When she described her wait to me, I was immediately reminded of the long lines at Soviet state stores that Ronald Reagan used to joke about. And then it occurred to me that we Americans have been conditioned to keep two separate clocks in our heads, a clock with a second hand for private transactions and a clock that moves only in fifteen-minute increments for government offices. If you think this is an exaggeration, pay attention to what happens to you the next few times you go out to spend your money voluntarily, and compare it with what happens when you go to a place you have been compelled to finance through your taxes. Write down exactly how long it took you to get impatient on each kind of errand. You might be surprised, or, on the other hand, you might not be surprised to discover how much more quickly you get impatient when you are a customer instead of a client.

If we are truly going to take advantage of the great opportunity before us, one of the first things we have to do is learn how to apply to the public sector the principles that have made the American economy the wonder of the world. There are a num-

ber of reasons that the private sector today is more open to the
needs of its customers and to the most effective methods of cutting costs and increasing productivity—why, in other words, it
has been able to adopt, and adapt, both the new time- and man-
power-saving techniques provided by technology and the new
management techniques for improving the performance of its
personnel. Naturally, the first and most important of these reasons is the bottom line. The more efficient and service-conscious
a supplier of goods is, the greater his profit.

But the public sector, too, ought to be considering its bottom
line, measured not in individual or corporate earnings but in
terms of meeting goals to ensure a safe, prosperous, healthy, and
free future for our children and grandchildren.

The transition from sixty years of deficit spending to this
new era of budget surpluses is a great opportunity for us, legislators and citizens together, to determine how we can reach the
goals I have just outlined. After all, in one way or another, virtually everyone in this country engages in some form of long-
range planning. People tell their children to do their homework
for the sake of the long-term benefits that will one day far out-
match the loss of the chance to watch television today. They buy
houses with twenty- or thirty-year mortgages because they
believe they will pay off in the long run. People go to college or
to vocational technical school because they know that in the
long run the advantage of their having done so will far outweigh
any temporary loss of income in the present. They take out student loans and repay them over a number of years (in my case,
fourteen) because they know that the debt they incur today will
bring an ultimate benefit far out of proportion to its cost.

In other words, investing for the future, whether they think
of it that way or not, is built into the psyches of virtually all

Americans. We need from now on to take a leaf from our personal book in thinking about and managing the affairs of government. Heretofore, too many people have been content to remain trapped in such short-term thinking as annual budgets or nine-second sound bites. In fact, what we need is a serious conversation about our national future between the overwhelming majority of ordinary Americans and those of us who have been given the priceless opportunity to serve them in public office.

The citizens of the United States of America are overwhelmingly committed to lives of faith, family, work, opportunity, and love of country. They know what they want, and what they want is precisely what we members of the entrepreneurial party are determined to help them achieve: a truly safe, secure, prosperous, and free future.

In 1994 they gave us 9 million additional votes in response to our announced intention to reform welfare, cut taxes, balance the budget, reform education, reduce regulation, free society from opportunistic litigation, and curtail the Internal Revenue Service. In 1996 the voters came to the conclusion that while we had made some mistakes, our hearts and minds were in the right place. Our majority survived a huge, very nasty, very expensive attack campaign against us. One of the things people most appreciated was our finally successful effort to reform the welfare system. They forgave us for quite a few of our beginners' mistakes in return for that long-desired reform of welfare. In 1997 we successfully picked up the pace of what is going to be a long but cheerful trek into a better future. There are many things left to do on this journey, some of them easy, just waiting to happen, and some of them requiring full-scale battle against entrenched bureaucracies acting in partnership with special interest groups and skillful at making use of the services of demagogues. Dealing with these opponents requires courage and intellectual strength. The issue, then, is not merely one of bigger government or smaller government, but of how to make government smarter, more cost-effective, and less destructive of human resources.

Consider the Earned Income Credit program, one of the biggest scandals in the Internal Revenue Service. This program provides cash payment to people below a certain income level. Clearly, it has become an invitation to fraud, and one that is accepted all too frequently. The Clinton Administration's own estimates of waste, fraud, and error indicate that the program has a 21 percent rate of error. That means that $1 out of every $5 distributed is wrong. There are big problems with a 21 percent error rate in a government program that gives away money. First, it teaches people to commit fraud. A society in which the dishonest gain more benefit than the honest is one whose very fabric is being frayed. Second, it points up a grotesque double standard in the inner workings of the IRS: When you send them your money, they punish you for anything less than 100 percent accuracy, but when they send your money to someone else, they accept their own massive error rate. Congressman Mike Crapo showed me an IRS letter to a retired judge of the Idaho Supreme Court who had underpaid his quarterly estimated taxes by 69 cents. They were demanding $123.01: $123 as a fine, and 1 cent in interest. The judge wondered, as well he might, if the government had lost its mind. What would he say if he were told that the IRS sends out an estimated $5 billion annually in wrong payments under the Earned Income Credit program? That is enough money to abolish the entire death tax. The earned income credit program was devised out of the best of motives—so that the working poor should not feel penalized for working by comparison with the welfare recipients. But with a high rate of fraud compounded by incompetence, it is worse than merely a well-meaning failure. If we must have such a program, it should be contracted out to Visa or MasterCard or American Express or some other sophisticated company that handles millions of accounts every month and refuses to accept more than a one-half or one percent rate of error. If contracting out is impossible, we should abolish the program. Under no circumstances should we accept the principle that it is okay to give away more than $5 billion a year to people who do not deserve it.

Take an entirely different example, one involving health. Diabetes affects 14 percent of all senior citizens, and medical care related to diabetes accounts for 27 percent of the total Medicare budget. It can lead to blindness, loss of kidney function, heart disease, and amputation of the feet and legs. Yet diabetes can be dramatically diminished as a threat to health by periodic testing and preventive education. The Centers for Disease Control (CDC) estimates that if people learn that they have diabetes and learn to monitor their blood sugar, control their diet, and generally take care of themselves, not only will their lives be immeasurably better, but we will save $14 billion a year. The CDC estimates we can save 90 percent of those who go blind and two-thirds of those who otherwise will lose their kidney or feet or suffer heart disease. Lives will be better. Budgets will be better. It is a win-win proposition.

Moreover, if diabetes is a problem for the population at large, it is a crisis for certain Native American tribes, among whom is found the largest concentration of diabetes per capita in the country. In some tribes the rate of the disease is 50 percent. The Indian Health Service, a badly run Washington bureaucracy, has done a terrible job. When I meet with tribal leaders, they are unanimous is requesting that the government take power away from the Washington bureaucracy and return it to their local communities. In 1997 we established a new diabetes program specifically for Native Americans. We are going to do all we can to make sure that the resources, very much including preventive care, are focused on the reservations. Health workers on the spot truly understand the problems and are passionate to do something about them. The 1997 Medicare reforms include the first steps toward the kind of preventive health program for the nation's diabetics that will ultimately save both lives and money.

Another, similar example is the opportunity we have now to preempt the coming crisis in Alzheimer's disease care, which in the twenty-first century is going to become one of our most expensive health problems. As people live longer and more of them are left with Alzheimer's, the requirements for full-time nursing care, expensive as they are now, are going to become even more so. For every dollar we invest now in biomedical research on this disease, we will save a thousand dollars or more in the next generation. Here is an example where leading by looking ahead we can avoid a crisis that is otherwise virtually guaranteed to happen.

These are only a few examples of the opportunities that are waiting, examples that come to mind because I have lately been preoccupied with them. There are many more. It is curious that opportunities of this kind seem to be invisible to much of the news media and many of our liberal friends. Indeed, it is ironic the way many liberals go to Russia, Korea, Indonesia, and Japan to urge free markets and government withdrawal from subsidies and controls. Yet as soon as they return to America, they forget their own advice. Here at home they advocate the expansion of

Washington-based programs with all their attendant bureaucracies and taxpayer subsidies.

We must have the honesty to apply here at home the same principles we preach abroad. We need to rethink each and every aspect of our bureaucratized government to make sure it is really necessary. If it is really necessary, is it being implemented as effectively as possible? Four tests will help us to accomplish this rethinking.

1: Have we included the enormous potential of new scientific discoveries and their accompanying technologies? Consider the new technologies in the field of communication. We are going through a transformation in our ability to do business, create wealth, deliver goods and services, and solve problems. That transformation should also affect our way of delivering government. We have barely begun to think through the implications of this technological transformation. The greatest gap in modern politics is our inability to explain and popularize the potential of the information age and turn it into practical programmatic realities. We are on the edge of a world of new opportunity, but we do not yet know how to describe it or how to organize it. That is the first and greatest challenge of our generation.

2: We must ask of every government effort: Is it really necessary for government to be engaged in this? Can it be accomplished better by private industry or business, by an independent nonprofit activity, or by volunteers and charities? The heart of American freedom and creativity was captured by de Tocqueville in his *Democracy in America* when he noted how volunteerism and local mediating institutions were the keys to the vitality of American society in the 1830s—an idea that has been rediscovered and given new life by Marvin Olasky and other critics of the welfare state in recent years.

3: If government ought to be responsible for a particular program or function, is it necessary that the program be centralized in Washington, or would society be better off if it were devolved to state and local government? There it would be closer to the needs and desires of the people, and there, too, the diversity of effort in all the various localities would increase the opportunity for entrepreneurial thinking and the application of innovative technologies. This is the essence of the efforts of Governor Mike Leavitt of Utah to have us reassert the Tenth Amendment to the Constitution. That amendment reserves to the states and the people therein all powers not expressly given to the federal government by the Constitution. It was added to the Constitution in the first place because the Founding Fathers wisely feared the possibility of the untrammeled growth of a centralized federal government.

4: If it is decided that only the federal government can be in charge of something, are we implementing the program with the best applicable new science and technology? Are we implementing it as cleanly and efficiently as possible, or is it being managed with waste, fraud, and incompetence?

These four questions capture the heart of a new system meant to replace the mind-set of welfare with the spirit of opportunity in the twenty-first century. If we pursue the potential inherent in each of these questions, we will find ourselves in a healthier and wealthier country. We will better be able to deal with its challenges at home and to be a confident major power in the world.

Each time we successfully bring about some needed change, our solution, by altering the world, *may* in turn create new complications. This is a healthy process, one not to be feared but rather to look forward to. At this moment, however, we are confronted with problems whose solution would actually spell a great new era in the life of this country as a whole and in the individual lives of its citizens. It is not often that people are given such an opportunity. We intend, with all the help we can get, from both voters as well as technical experts, to get the job done.

It is essential that we find the means to create a drug-free society for our children. As everyone knows, this has not been an easy matter for us. There are societies that have successfully beaten the drug culture, Singapore and Malaysia being prime examples. But while driving out drug use, we need to be more protective of individual freedom than they have been. We ourselves dramatically reduced drug use in the 1920s, soon after World War I, and for forty years drugs were used only on the margins of our society.

The Partnership for a Drug-Free America, with its constant efforts at persuasion and education, and Nancy Reagan's "Just Say No" campaign had a real effect on drug use between 1984 and 1992. In fact, drug use declined by two-thirds in eight years. Drug use began to rise again when the educational ad campaigns were dumped by the Clinton Administration. Now we have to launch a full-scale torrent of antidrug education, in schools, in churches, in youth organizations, in after-school programs, and everywhere else that young people hang out. We must also raise the cost of buying and using drugs. The problem does not stem from Mexico or Colombia, but from the neighborhoods in America where drugs are being used. We must find a number of economic and social penalties—not just the threat of prison which we know does not work—that will make drug use socially unacceptable. But as regards drug dealers and especially the organizations at the top of the drug-distribution pyramid, we have to prove our absolute determination to save our children's lives. Anyone convicted of importing a commercial quantity of drugs should be given a mandatory life sentence. If it is proven beyond a reasonable doubt that their importations have caused the addiction and death of any American children, a death sentence should be mandatory.

Another thing we must do is seal off the American border by combining the Border Patrol, the Customs Service, and the Immigration and Naturalization Service into one focused border agency. Wherever there are large numbers of illegals trying to cross, we should install triple fencing, and at all official crossings, we should install sophisticated drug detection equipment. Any foreign government that is willing to take on the drug dealers, growers, and processors should be given all our support— exactly as if it were a wartime ally. We should see to it that being on the side of the United States in opposing the drug trade should be a very advantageous policy for any country.

While we are doing all this, we must initiate an all-out effort to get current addicts off drugs. Finally, we have to take back our prisons, with weekly drug testing and mandatory education and work programs designed to turn back out on the street people who are drug-free and have the ability to earn an honest living.

Another goal we must set ourselves is to ensure that every American has access to the best system of education and learning in the world. When I say everyone, I mean adults as well as children. The changes being wrought by the information age combined with a genuine world marketplace are going to demand of people a constant process of learning. People who learn all their lives will be those most rewarded by the market. Notice I have used both the words "education" and "learning," for both are important but they are very different things. A system of education is a structure controlled by educators and entered at their convenience to teach you what they value and believe you ought to know; whereas learning is a process you enter into yourself at your convenience to acquaint yourself with, or perhaps to master, something you wish or need to know.

The industrial age was the great age of education, public schools were invented by a society that built factories, and psychologically they are deeply related as to structure. The information age, however, will be the great age of systems of learning. Public libraries are a kind of early preelectronic precursor of the world that is being born. Already one can access electronically, on a twenty-four-hour-a-day, seven-day-a-week basis, vast systems of knowledge and information, and it will not be that long before doing so will be as commonplace as, say, using the telephone. The really great breakthroughs in learning will occur in the home and office rather than the school.

Our present-day school systems are often impediments to education as well as to learning, but especially to the latter. In our poorest neighborhoods are our poorest schools, measured in student achievement. (They are certainly not our poorest measured in money spent per pupil. On the contrary. In Washington, D.C., for instance, where many schools have simply appalling records of achievement, the annual expenditure per pupil is approximately $10,000—among the highest in the land.) As a consequence, many of today's schoolchildren are being cheated of the opportunity ever to enter a system of learning, graduating from high school yet barely able to read or write. We owe it not only to our children but to the future of our country to insist that they be given a real education, and beyond this, that there be a well-developed system of learning for Americans of all ages.

Every child of every background in every neighborhood has been endowed by our Creator with the unalienable right to pursue happiness. A basic education is the very foundation of the ability to pursue happiness in the information age. Hence to receive one is every child's right. In 1983 a report on the condition of the schools called *A Nation at Risk* was produced for President Reagan. It said what many people knew and many others could no longer deny, namely, that all too many of our schools were failing. After that, a host of study commissions, academic reports, and foundation projects were devoted to this problem. What followed were a host of excuses. What did not follow was the scale of change we need for our children's sake.

In World War II Winston Churchill devised for himself a technique to get the bureaucracy moving. He would attach a preprinted slip that read "Action This Day" to every document he regarded as urgent. This is what we must do about all those children whose lives may be wasted, or at least made unfairly difficult, in the present system of schooling. The task will involve a variety of "actions this day." To begin with, we have to establish a national goal—that every child be able to read and write English by the end of the first grade. We should resolve that anyone who is already above the first grade should adopt this as an immediate goal and should be immersed in achieving it. And following from this, we should also build a literacy learning system for illiterate adults. I do not mean by this that we need a new federal law. Rather, we need a commitment of the American people expressed through their local school boards and state legislatures.

State legislatures should see to it that one day each school year be devoted by every grade level to studying the Declaration of Independence and the Constitution. While teachers are teaching this, among other things they will have to explain what the Founding Fathers meant by the Creator, that it is through Him that we have been endowed with rights and thus to Him that we are ultimately responsible. Beyond this essential reminder of our grounding as one nation under God, an annual study of the Declaration and the Constitution will serve as a reminder of the romance, power, and political brilliance of the founders of the American system. Young Americans will learn why America has been the freest and most stable system on the planet for over two hundred years.

We should encourage the spread of public charter schools, one of the happiest new developments on the education scene, so parents, educators, and students working together can enjoy the maximum freedom to be enterprising, to explore options and innovations until every child has a genuine opportunity to learn. As a corollary of this, we must identify the worst schools. We should insist on immediate change for bad schools. To start with, there should be no tenure and no binding contracts in the worst 20 percent of schools. If, say, we were systematically being cheated by the employees of McDonald's or Wal-Mart, we would expect management to change the system immediately. The same principle should apply to schools that are failing to educate the children they serve.

If, despite all this, there were families left without an acceptable local public school, scholarships should be available for them to find a private one. I am a graduate of a public school, as are my wife and my two daughters. All of us remain committed to the idea of public education. However, if the available public school is one that gives parents legitimate worry for their children's future, there ought to be an alternative to having to stand by helplessly watching an incompetent bureaucracy destroy their children's lives.

Another urgent task is to create new alternatives for retirement before the system we have now collapses under the weight of the baby boomers. The social security system was originally based on the principle of a low rate of return per dollar invested because there were so many workers and so few retirees that the system could transfer wealth from the worker to the retiree without anyone noticing or complaining. It was fine for 1935, when it was devised, but now we are entering a very different era. The generation known as the baby boomers is so big that if we retain the 1935 system, the boomers will bankrupt the retirement system their children and grandchildren will turn to in about thirty years. Indeed, their children and grandchildren may actually end up with a negative rate of return on their FICA taxes. In other words, anyone young today may not only get a bad rate of return, he or she may actually get back less than he or she pays in. Many Americans under thirty simply take for granted that the system will collapse before they reach retirement.

Furthermore, the real cost of the current system to the individual is hidden because the law was written so that the employer is required to split the tax with you. This, of course, is a fiction. Virtually every labor economist in America agrees that the employee pays the entire tax. After all, if the employee was not earning the money with which the employer pays the tax, the employer would not keep them on.

One of the simple steps we need to take is to amend the law so that an individual's paycheck reflects the amount of money that is actually being paid into the FICA system. People will soon begin to realize that they are paying twice the tax they had originally believed they were paying. For over half the American population the total FICA tax they are paying is bigger than their income tax.

We are now able to develop a new, personal, modern, social security system. For one thing, information technology now makes it possible to handle each person's retirement account separately. For another, the growing understanding that the system we have is in crisis makes people more willing to discuss new proposals than they used to be. Not that many years ago, few people who understood the true, underlying predicament of the social security system dared to be candid about it in public. It is still considered too risky by many politicians. In our present situation, our ability to keep track of individual accounts combined with the power of compound interest creates the possibility for new workers to have four or five times as much money for their retirement as they would have if we kept the present system going. One estimate is that for a twenty-year-old today, a system of individual retirement accounts would provide $975,000 in retirement as compared with the current system's $175,000. Why would anyone wish to cheat a young person out of the possibility of one day having an additional $800,000?

The first thing we have to do is establish a National Commission on Retirement. One-third of its members should be baby boomers, one-third should be older, and one-third younger. We need an intergenerational dialogue to avoid the danger of intergenerational conflict. In addition to this, every member of the House and Senate should be encouraged to set up local citizens' committees to rethink retirement. These local committees should be connected to the National Commission by the Internet, so that as the National Commission develops research and proposals they would automatically be disseminated to each of the local committees. The local committees could forward ideas and questions to the National Commission. Thus the conversation on this subject would genuinely be a national one. Such a national dialogue, moreover, should continue for a year so that everyone can come to accept a common set of facts and raise every issue that worries them or causes them genuine fear. There has never been a national dialogue like this, but we have to have faith that the same citizens who buy their own cars, buy their own houses, and choose their own elected leaders can be just as much trusted as their leaders to think their way through a retirement system that will sooner or later affect the lives of every single one of them.

Now is the moment. Our transition from a government in deficit to one of surplus gives us the opportunity as never before to think about the future without having to play a zero-sum game over the future of the American people. We can use some of our surpluses to redeem the social security bonds so that we will be able to redeem our debt to older Americans without bankrupting younger ones. We are currently far enough ahead of the real crisis point of social security (which will occur around 2027) to be able to design and begin to carry out the change needed to put the system on an even keel and guarantee our country's young a decent retirement.

Whenever this issue comes up in Washington, one immediately begins to hear the words "hard choices" and "pain." This is a sign of how little some of our pundits understand about the potent combination of compound interest and economic growth. If we act with genuinely good sense in the near future, everyone, from senior citizens to baby boomers to those in their first jobs, can come out a winner with a safe, secure, better retirement program.

Finally, there should be a national standard for how much the government should be allowed to take out of our pockets in peacetime. America was founded as a country with the least taxed citizens in the world. We have spent a good part of our history being just that. The way now for us to be able to ensure and remain the country with the greatest, most productive, and most reliable wealth-making private sector is once again to limit the greed of government.

Today government at all levels, federal, state, and local, soaks up about 38 percent of our income, 22 percent of that for the federal government and 16 percent on average for the state and local governments. I believe we should set the peacetime limit on taxes from all levels of government combined at 25 percent. Taxes would go down as spending went down.

This should not, however, be done by passing a federal law. As with social security reform, I think we must have a national dialogue and build a national majority for these goals. Each level of government would then have to do its part to achieve them. Such a reduction in government and taxes would probably take a decade or more to bring about. It would also be a reflection of other efforts to shrink government and pay down the national debt, such as were undertaken by the Jeffersonians, the Jacksonians, the Republicans after the Civil War, and again after World War I.

We have just finished a half-century during which we won

World War II and then the Cold War. It is natural in wartime for government to get bigger. Now we are at the edge of what might well be a long period of peace. This peace will be truly stable if we have the best system of learning and education in the world, the largest economy in the world, and the necessary ingredients for keeping us the only superpower in the world. We can keep the peace by remaining strong beyond any challenge. That does not mean that there will be no more minor or secondary conflicts. There will always be those. But with a strong economy and a sufficiently strong military, they should not affect our civilian stability.

Imagine an America which is drug- and violence-free; in which every citizen of every age has full access to the best system of education and learning in the world; in which every individual has a retirement system that promises him or her a long life with genuine dignity and comfort; and in which a modernized, efficient government took only one-quarter of one's income.

In 1994 we Republicans said we could balance the budget, cut taxes, reform welfare, help the poor move from welfare to work and thus from poverty to prosperity. We said we could save Medicare by increasing choices for the consumer and putting greater emphasis on preventive health measures. We can now say that we kept that faith.

The coming years will provide us with a great opportunity to have a dialogue about our future among the country's citizens and to set ourselves goals for a generation. There is something to learn every day. With what we learn we can build a healthier and happier America for our children and grandchildren. Who can ask for more than that?

Index